About The Author

CLYDE ORMOND lives in Rigby, Idaho, on the land his father once homesteaded. Formerly a school teacher and principal, and for the past thirty years a prolific outdoor writer, he has hunted and fished over most of North America and has guided others on trips into wilderness regions.

OUTDOORSMAN'S HANDBOOK

Clyde Ormond

Edited by Henry Gross

Illustrated by Nicholas Alnorosi

A BERKLEY WINDHOVER BOOK

published by

BERKLEY PUBLISHING CORPORATION

To My Wife,

Lucille Anderson Ormond

Contents

How to Make an Elk Bugle • How to Make a Moose Call • Varmint Calls • Rattling Up a Buck • Handling Guns Safely • Installing Scope Sights • Installing Sling Swivels • Installing a New Stock • Finishing a Stock • Cleaning Guns in an Emergency • Sighting-In a Rifle • Simple Shooting Bench • Fore-End Rest • Sandbags • Backstop • Sighting-In Targets • Shotgun Targets • Shortening and Crowning a Rifle Barrel • Thwarting Condensation • Storing Guns at Camp • Reloading Ammunition • Light Rifle Sling • The Rifle Scabbard • Simple Duck and Goose Decoys • Estimating Bird Flocks • Blinds • Hanging Heavy Deer • Simple Game Hoist • Buttonholing a Deer • Packing Elk Quarters • Skidding and Travois • Scalding Chicken or Grouse • Skinning Big Game for Trophies • Skinning Furred Animals • Skinning Birds • How to Make an Indian Hide Frame •

Cutting Out the Antler Plate • Skinning a Canine's Tail •
Keeping Meat in Hot Weather • By-Products of the
Hunt • Bear Fat For Boots • How Indians Made
Arrowheads

Part 2 — Fishing How-To   83

Emergency Fishing Kit • Tying Emergency Flies •
Tying Flies at Camp • Painting Metal Lures • Emer-
gency Landing Net • Tying Tapered Leaders • Dropper
Loop • Splicing a Fly Line • Weighing a Fish with a
String • Measuring a Fish with Your Hand • Cleaning
Fish • Keeping Fish Cool • Making Sinkers • Replacing
Guides • Replacing a Tip Guide • Lubricating Ferrules •
Finding Natural Baits • Removing Embedded Fish-
hooks • How Indians Caught Fish • Indian Fish Wheel •
How Indians Dried Fish

Part 3 — Camping How-To   115

Making a Safe Camp • Keeping Matches Dry •
Fire Starters • Sharpening Axes and Knives • Chopping
Wood Safely • Splitting Wood • Sawing Wood • Camp
Cupboards • Camp Tables • Camp Stools • Homemade
Baker Tent • Lantern Case • Alforjas Boxes • Pack-
horse or Car Kitchen • Emergency Jack • Saw-Blade
Covers • Making Ax Sheaths • Knife Sheaths • Emer-
gency Needle • Tent Bags • Bough Bed • Leaf Bed •
Grass-and-Pole Bed • Dead-Man Tent Stakes • Trench-
ing a Tent • How to Dispose of Garbage • Camp Toilet-
Paper Holder • Simple Camp Utensils • Camp Tongs •
Doodle Hook • Walloper • Camp Toaster • Grub List •
Using a Space Blanket • Transplanting Trees and
Shrubs • How to Bank a Campfire • How Indians Car-
ried Fire • Plastic Water Carrier • Using Clorox Bottles •
Camp Coat Hangers • Hauling Ice Water in a Car •

Indian Tipis and Wigwams • Indian Steam Bath • How Indians Made Rabbit-Skin Blankets • Driving a Nail with a Handkerchief

Part 8 — Miscellaneous How-To   297

Foreword

By Don Samuelson
Governor of Idaho

If the best things in life are free, as the bards and ballad writers say, then the magnificent outdoors and the pure pleasures it provides ranks right at the top of life's blessings. The outdoors belong to everyone. It is a part of our precious American heritage — a heritage we must conserve and protect and pass on to future generations.

Clean air and clean water in a clean environment must be among the foremost goals of this nation. Uncontaminated areas must be kept that way. Where pollution has fouled the air or water, restoration to cleanliness must be undertaken vigorously and promptly.

Here in Idaho, as in most other Western states, pollution is a critical and severe problem only in a few scattered regions. Concentrated and firm steps have already been taken to alleviate and eventually eliminate air and water pollutants in affected areas, with rigid and stringent prohibitions against creation of any new problem areas.

Man, wherever he lives, is entitled to breathe clean air and to drink clean water. I hope the recent surge of interest and concern in environment and clean air and clean water is maintained on an enduring basis.

I noted above that the outdoors belongs to everyone.

In some special illustrious cases, the reverse of that statement also is true, and applies here to Clyde Ormond, the author of this knowledgeable book, which I predict will be considered a masterpiece in its field. Because Clyde Ormond belongs to the outdoors.

I know from a personal warm friendship of twenty-five years that Clyde's romance with and devotion to the lure and splendor of the outdoors qualifies him as well as anybody in the United States to write this book.

Along with millions of other Americans from all fifty states, I consider myself an outdoorsman, too. Along the way, I acquired a fair amount of expertise and an enduring admiration and love of nature's constant appeal and attraction. I bow to the master craftsman — Clyde Ormond — because here is a sportsman who I am sure has spent more time outdoors than in. I suspect that if Clyde had his way, the only roof he would ever want over his head would be a sky full of sunshine during the day and starshine at night.

Clyde Ormond's qualifications to write this handbook are impeccable, simply because he is an outdoorsman who is an acknowledged authority on the many subjects included in the following pages. I'm glad he's decided to share his life in the great outdoors with others, because a mighty lot of people are going to get a mighty lot of information out of this book.

Outdoorsman's Handbook

Introduction

Because of the increasing complexities of day-to-day living, and the growing shift toward urbanization, man's real need of the outdoors has intensified. Amid rugged mountains, rushing rivers, and peaceful forests, one leaves the cares of the world behind. The heart and mind are soothed, the spirit ennobled.

A great part of enjoying the outdoor experience depends on man's ability to adapt to this simple environment. In the outdoors, the conveniences of home are left behind. In place of the gadgets created by man's ingenuity, there is only the natural world—its plants, rocks, and animals—to satisfy his needs. Here there are many new and exciting challenges. Inability to respond to these challenges—to invent, to adapt, to improvise—inevitably detracts from one's enjoyment and often jeopardizes one's safety.

Camping trips are spoiled by someone's inability to build a fire with wet wood. Fishing trips are spoiled when tackle is lost and the angler lacks the know-how to make substitute lures from materials at hand. Hunting trips are spoiled when a hunter pokes his rifle barrel in the mud and doesn't know how to clean the bore without a cleaning rod.

This book attempts to fill a long-standing need for a compact source of information to help outdoorsmen solve many of the problems and challenges they encounter on their excursions. The hundreds of tips and techniques in this volume were collected over a lifetime of hunting, fishing, and camping across North America in the company of mountain men, wilderness guides, and the greatest woodsmen of all, the Indians. In passing along this fund of lore to my fellow outdoorsmen, I hope to keep alive this hard-won knowledge and to inspire others to tax their ingenuity and imagination in further ways.

PART 1

Hunting How-To

How to Make an Elk Bugle

One of the most thrilling forms of hunting is bugle-ing for elk. Bull elk will answer the call of another bull during the rutting season, and this call can be simulated with a bamboo bugle. To use a bugle effectively requires a knowledge of the bull's mating call and the behavior at this time of the year.

The best bugles are made of node-free bamboo, of a length and diameter that will produce the four, distinct, arpeggio-like tones of the bull's bugling. The ideal size is 17 inches in length with an outside diameter of 1 inch.

Cut the bamboo to length and scrape the fuzz from the inside with fine sandpaper on a dowel. With a fine-toothed backsaw make a cut approximately 1½ inches from the open end, to a depth of about one-third the bamboo's diameter. Then, with a knife, make a slanting cut an inch from the saw cut, forming a notch.

Next, make a wooden plug that will fit snugly into the notched end of the bugle. Make this plug of a relatively hard wood; soft wood will absorb moisture and ruin the tone. The end of a broom handle makes a fine plug. This plug should be the same length as the distance from the blowing end to the notch. It should be sanded smooth and fit snugly. Then shave the top of the plug flat along its full length. This permits air to be blown into the bugle. Shave the plug cautiously, cutting down only enough to get the needed air passage.

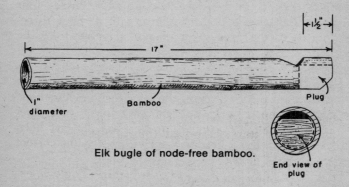

Elk bugle of node-free bamboo.

By continued trial—pushing the plug farther in or pulling it out a trifle—you will find that the bugle can be blown. This is accomplished by blowing into the plug end and holding the hand over the other end. If it won't whistle, push the plug in or back it out a little. At some point, if everything is right, the bugle will produce a whistle. If you blow harder, you can make higher-pitched notes or tones, just as a bugler can, by tightening his lips, produce several tones without any keys. You will find that you can make four distinct tones, like a musical arpeggio. If you can make only two or three, shift the plug, or flatten the top, or deepen the notch a trifle.

When you can make four tones, mark the position of the plug with a knife scratch so it can be replaced in the identical position. Then, if the blowing end is too big for your mouth, cut the lower edge on a slant—so that it resembles the top of a saxophone mouthpiece. Finally, coat the plug with airplane cement and replace it. It's smart at this stage to give it one more toot, to make certain it is tuned right, before the cement dries.

The finished bugle should sound something like this: "Da-da-da-deeeeeee-da-da-dum!" These four tones imitate the bull's bugling, with at least three-fourths of the time spent on note number four, the highest tone.

As good bamboo is becoming hard to obtain, an adequate bugle also can be made of ⅝-inch plastic garden hose. It won't have the same deep, mellow tone of the bamboo bugle, but will work fairly well, especially on bulls in primitive areas which haven't been overhunted. For a hose of ⅝-inch diameter, the correct length is 14 inches.

This bugle is made just as a bamboo bugle is, except that the end plug doesn't have to be cemented. It is shaped round, and should be friction-tight. The plastic seals it.

In an emergency, a form of elk bugle can be made of two empty cartridge cases of different size. One should be small. The two cases are taped together with adhesive tape, edge-to-edge. The larger case is blown into first, since it will make the deeper tone. Then the smaller case is blown into for a longer period, simulating the high-pitched tone. A .38 Special revolver case and a .338 Magnum rifle case will make a crude bugle. It will often work on unalerted bulls.

How to Make a Moose Call

The Indians used to make moose calls of birchbark, and the technique is useful today. The Indian call was made in the shape of a small horn or megaphone,

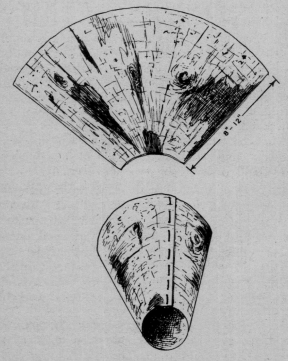

Birchbark moose call.

ranging from 8 to 12 inches in length. The pattern for this resembled a fan, extended so that it covered one-third of a complete circle. The edges of the bark were then overlapped and stitched down with cord, sinew, or buckskin.

To use such a call, place it over the lips and make a grunting sound—"Uh-waugh! Uh-waugh!" Rapidly expelling a lungful of air helps. This resembles the love call of a moose in the rut, and through the funnel-like call will carry for a considerable distance in calm evening air. You can make such a call of bark, or of a section of a cardboard carton.

Lacking either bark or cardboard, you can simply cup your hands over your mouth as when shouting. Each guttural sound is made with the cupped hands half closed for the first syllable, then opened widely for the second part—much as a trombonist opens the mute on the end of his instrument.

Varmint Calls

The purpose of a varmint call is to simulate the scream of a dying or caught rabbit and lure a varmint in the area within shooting range. You can make a simple varmint call from two slats of softwood, one or two wide rubber bands, and some adhesive tape.

The best wood for this call is a 3-foot yardstick available at any lumberyard. Such a yardstick is approximately ³⁄₁₆ inch thick and of easily workable wood.

Saw two slats from the yardstick ¾ inch wide and 6 inches long. At the center of each slat, hollow out the face for 2 inches along the length to a depth of about ¹⁄₁₆ inch at the center.

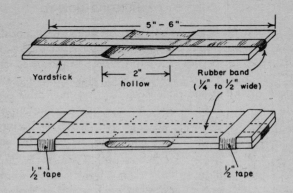

 Varmint call made from two lengths of yardstick and rubber band.

Next, either one or two rubber bands of ¼ to ½ inch width (depending on the quality of tone desired), and 5 inches in length, are stretched tightly around the top slat. When this top slat is placed over the lower slat, there will be a thin, elliptical opening at the center. The rubber band(s) will run across this opening. To complete the call, tape both ends of the slats tightly together about 1 inch from each end.

The finished call is held edgewise in the mouth, like a thin harmonica. The sound is made by blowing through it, against the edge of the taut rubber bands. With practice, and by cupping and opening the hands about the call as it is played, you can create the most unearthly yowls imaginable and can simulate the cry of a caught rabbit. The sound from this call will carry unbelievable distances, especially in still air. The point to remember is that the pitch of the sound is determined by the tension of the rubber bands, which in turn is determined by their length. For a higher pitch use a shorter, or tighter, band, and vice versa.

A simpler varmint call can be made with nothing more than a blade of large, tough grass. To make this call, place the hands with the palms together so that the two thumbs lie edgewise and parallel. The palms should be mildly cupped. With the thumbs in this position, they are bent slightly downward into the cupped hands. The blade of grass is placed edgewise between the thumbs, being held at one end between the nails and the first joint, and at the other end by the meaty portion at the second joint.

With the blade edgewise and taut, place the mouth over the opening between the thumbs, and blow hard. You'll make some weird and awesome screeches before you learn to regulate the tension of the grass blade and can simulate the cry of a trapped rabbit. The first coyote I ever called within rifle shot was coaxed with this type of varmint call.

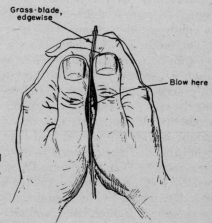

Grass-blade, edgewise

Blow here

Grass blade used as a varmint call.

Rattling up a Buck

The best way to learn to rattle up a deer is to watch a buck rub off the summer's velvet, and polish his antlers, against a suitable tree. If these sounds—the swishing, banging, huffing, and rattling— could be put on tape, then somehow simulated, rattling would be comparatively easy. And, if the actual sounds of two bucks fighting could be heard, artificially duplicating those sounds would be simple.

First it is necessary to find a pair of shed deer antlers. Whitetail antlers should be used for rattling a whitetail buck. Old-timers at the game say that one-year-old antlers are best if they can be found, for they still have the crispness of live antlers.

Take the pair of antlers to a deer area, and station yourself in an opening in heavy foliage. One hunter can work alone, or two can be together—one to rattle, the other to shoot if and when a buck appears. Both should wear camouflage clothing to match the surroundings.

Holding an antler in each hand, bang them together as if two bucks charged each other head-on. Then twist and rattle them as if the bucks were disengaging their headgear. After a slight pause, rake an antler against a tree a few times. Then bang them together again. Next, rake one of antlers noisily over rocks. Repeat this sequence for up to a half minute, then remain silent, and listen. Naturally, you should be downwind from the direction you expect a buck might appear.

After ten minutes, if no buck shows up, move to another part of the opening (as though two fighting bucks might move) and repeat the performance. Always remain at the edge of the opening, not out in the open.

If there is a rutting buck in the area, and the rattling has authentically simulated two bucks fighting, or one scraping velvet off his antlers, he's apt to come out of curiosity or pugnacity.

I have repeatedly watch experienced hunters rattle for a buck in the whitetail country of Texas; and their performance, as they banged antlers together, moved off and raked them against brush, and got down on their knees to grunt and rake the dry antlers over patches of rocks, would rival the most imaginative Indian ceremonial show. But these hunters had rattled up bucks many times. One told me that once while he was on his knees, scraping on the rocks, "—a buck with horns like the Charter Oak jumped clean into the openin', and almost lit on top of me. I was so scared I couldn't shoot!"

Handling Guns Safely

There are many specific do's and don'ts about gun handling which, if followed, will prevent gun accidents. These rules, which have been time- and field-tested, are especially useful for the beginning shooter.

I have found a single rule which, if religiously followed, will prevent gun accidents. "Never point a gun at a human being."

But this simple rule needs some explanation. It does not mean merely to avoid pointing a gun at a person when hunting. It means that even when handling and transporting guns they should not be pointed at someone.

Guns should not be carried so their muzzles point in a lateral direction—somewhere in the distance there may be a person. Instead, guns in the hunting field and elsewhere should be carried with muzzles either up or down. Similarly, guns should not be transported in vehicles on a seat in horizontal position. Guns should be transported in vehicles with muzzles pointed upward or downward.

Guns should not be placed muzzle up against a slender tree, post, or fencewire. They may fall over and point toward a person. This applies as well to the rifle carried in a saddle scabbard. It should never be carried horizontally alongside the saddle, but with the muzzle pointed either up or down.

If you examine this simple rule, in every aspect of its application, you'll find that it embraces almost every field situation; and that if the rule is rigidly applied it will largely do away with gun accidents.

There are of course many more gun rules dictated by common sense:

Do not clean a gun unless the action is open.

Keep ammunition locked up away from small children.

Don't try to shoot out obstructions from gun barrels.

Make certain the caliber or gauge of cartridges matches the gun to be used.

But the rule of never allowing a gun to be pointed at a human being, in all its applications, is the one rule that will cover most situations and prevent the most accidents.

Installing Scope Sights

The average shooter or hunter, if he is at all handy with simple tools, can install his own scope. Today's standard factory or custom rifles come already drilled and tapped for scope sights—that is, the receiver bridges and barrels are drilled for scope bases which have become standardized and will fit a variety of popular bases. These bases, in turn, will accept what have now become standardized diameters of scope tubes.

The tools needed for installing a scope are a couple of screwdrivers, an ordinary hammer, and a flat-ended punch.

If shop screwdrivers are used, make certain the ends are square and the sides are flat. This can be done by filing them, or grinding them on a small emery wheel. A screwdriver whose surfaces are not flat will jump from a screw head under tension and mar the looks of the job. One screwdriver should be small enough to fit the base screws and tightening screws of the scope itself. The other should fit larger screw knobs which hold the scope bands together.

Standard factory rifles come equipped with open sights. Some of these rifles will accept modern scope sights without removing the rear or the front sight, or both. Although the open sights protrude into a scope's line of sight, they will in actual use be blurred and will not interfere.

If it is necessary to remove an open sight, the hammer and small punch are needed. This punch may be a tiny brass plug about an inch long and ⅜ inch wide, designed for the purpose. Or a 16d nail, cut off to leave a 2 inch shank and filed square at the end, may be used. A square-end shop punch of suitable size is adequate. Place the punch on the base of the open sight as the rifle is held in a firm position horizontally. In this position, hit the punch sharply with the hammer, using a crisp, short stroke. It should move laterally in the barrel slot in which it has been fitted. A few more strokes with the hammer will punch out the sight base from the slot.

The important thing to remember in doing this is that such standard open sights are fitted into the barrel slots from the *right* side of the rifle, as the muzzle points away. Therefore, to remove the base requires that it be pounded out from the *left* side, since the barrel slots are midly tapered in dovetailing them.

The bottom of the scope bases, and that part of the rifle where they will be fastened, should be wiped free of all grease. If this job is completed with a slightly oiled cloth, all grease will be removed, but enough oil film will remain to prevent future rusting. The four tiny screws should be removed before doing this, and the tapped holes wiped free of all grease until perfectly dry. This can be done with a cloth on the end of a toothpick or match. Otherwise the base screws will tend to loosen with use.

The scope bases then are fitted and screwed to the receiver. Do not completely tighten the first screw of a base element before setting the second screw; then tighten both screws. The screws will withstand a firm turn with the screwdriver.

Next, fit the two scope rings around the scope tube and only partially tighten the setscrews, allowing the scope to turn within the rings. This allows positioning the scope correctly, but with enough tension so that it won't move unless desired. Now set the scope and rings into the bases, and partially tighten the large screws which hold the bands to the bases.

At this point, the scope rings and bases are firm enough so they won't move, but the scope tube itself will turn, under hand pressure, within the scope bands. This is necessary to adjust the scope so that its reticle will not cant, and to obtain proper eye-relief.

I have found the easiest way to rotate the scope so that it won't cant is simply to set the rifle in a solid

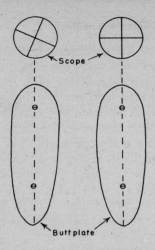

Align buttplate and scope reticle to correct cant. Scope at left is out of line.

position as in shooting; then, with the eye just a few inches behind the buttplate, move it up and down between scope reticle and buttplate. If the line between the center of the reticle and the buttplate appears to be straight, there will be no cant. Also, it is a good idea to aim through the scope at this point along the vertical line of a building or door jam. Any deviation from true vertical can be detected, and this will also disclose if you tend to hold the buttplate a bit off vertical.

Eye-relief is the distance between a shooter's eye and the scope, in a position where he can get a full field of view. It averages in most scopes from 3 to 5 inches.

To get proper eye-relief, place the rifle at the shoulder in actual shooting position, with your face on the comb of the stock where it will be during actual use. With the rifle in this position, move the scope gently back and forth within the bands until a full field of view is achieved.

Occasionally, owing to the combination of rifle, scope, mounts, and individual shooter, it is not possible to get a completely full field of view. Also, with rifles of very heavy recoil, it is wise to move the scope beyond which a full field of view occurs, in order to keep your eye from getting bumped in an awkward shooting position. This is not too important—the rifle will shoot just as straight, but it's a little harder to shoot quickly.

One final important detail: In rotating and setting the scope, be sure that the elevation-adjustment knob is on top of the scope—not on the left with the windage knob on top. If this occurs, sighting-in will be extremely difficult.

With this done, tighten all screws in both scope and anchoring elements, each one a little at a time. Tightening all screws on the right side before tightening any on the left will cause the scope to rotate slightly to the right, producing a bit of cant.

Installing Sling Swivels

A sling on a hunting rifle is used ninety-nine percent of the time for lugging the rifle around, and one percent when actually shooting. For this reason alone, any hunting rifle should be equipped with a sling—it takes most of the drudgery out of carrying a rifle.

Almost all modern rifles come equipped from the factory with sling swivels. For those not so equipped, it is easy to put on sling swivels. The tools needed are a brace and bit and a large screwdriver.

After removing the stock from the barreled action, place it in some form of vise which will hold it solidly.

Set the stock into the vise jaws between two strips of soft wood covered with cloth. This prevents marring the stock finish. The stock is placed upside down.

To set the rear swivel, mark a point with the end of a punch 2½ to 3 inches from the toe of the stock, exactly in the center. The distance depends upon preference, individual body size, and the overall length of the rifle. With a carbine or very short rifle, the distance from swivel to toe is less. This is where the rear swivel will be set.

A standard form of swivel, especially for the do-it-yourselfer, consists of a loop and screw as the rear element and a loop, screw, and nut for the fore-end.

The screw on the rear swivel tapers to a point and has deep, widely spaced threads. To set this swivel, it is only necessary to bore a hole in the stock with a bit whose diameter is slightly smaller than the swivel screw. When beginning to bore, make sure that the bit does not slip off the edge of the stock. Too large a bit will allow the swivel screw to slip out and loosen with use. And if the bit slips off, the stock will be marred. It is wise to experiment with the bit size on a piece of scrap wood. You then can tell if the fit will be snug enough, without splitting the stock. Bore the hole only a little at a time, testing the depth by pushing a match into the hole, holding a thumbnail at its depth, and comparing with the length of the swivel screw.

When the hole is the right depth, the swivel screw may be turned in until the base sets firmly upon the stock. Slip a screwdriver blade through the swivel loop to turn the screw flush.

The fore-end swivel is set similarly, except that two holes are bored. The first hole is placed at a point 2½ to 4 inches down from the fore-end tip—this, as mentioned, according to personal preference and rifle

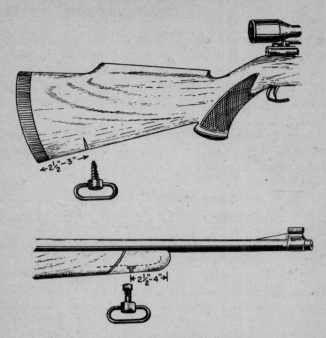

Installing sling swivels in stock and fore-end.

length. This hole is bored with a bit of the same diameter as the swivel screw. The screw on this element will not fit into the wood itself, like the rear swivel, but into a nut inside the barrel channel. This is a round nut, of the escutcheon type, and will bind into the wood of a larger hole.

The first hole is bored through the stock's center, all the way into the barrel channel. Next, a second hole is bored, from the inside of the barrel channel, to a depth that will allow the nut to be countersunk far enough into the wood so that, when the barrel is refitted, the nut and the barrel will not touch. This is determined by boring a little at a time, and trial and error. If the two touch, the rifle will shoot high.

Care should be used in boring this countersunk hole to make sure it is concentric with the first hole. Otherwise, the holes will be off-center and the screw won't fit.

The final step is to place the nut firmly into its fitting hole, carefully pushing the swivel screw through from the stock's outside, and turning it down tight. The rifle is then reassembled.

Other types of swivels, having different styles of bases, are installed in a comparable manner. With any type, it is important to test the boring and fit first with a piece of similar scrap wood. It's hard to undo a botched job on a fine gunstock.

Installing a New Stock

There are several reasons why you may want to put a new stock on a rifle. You may wish to modernize a military arm or to restore an old or prized piece. Or you may accidentally break a stock while hunting and want to replace it.

The advent of machine-inletted stocks on a mass, commercial basis made it possible for the average person to do this, when previously it was next to impossible. At one time, stockmaking involved cutting the blank from suitable timber, seasoning the wood plank, marking out a design, and then tediously carving, whittling, gouging, and chiseling until the stock was complete. Today, when a stockmaker says that his inletted blanks are "ninety percent completed," he means just that. Some need only sanding and finishing.

It is best for the average person with ordinary skill with tools to begin by restocking a bolt-action rifle. He can then graduate to other types of stocks, such as the fore-ends of shotguns, stocks for lever-action rifles, etc.

It is important when ordering an inletted blank to obtain the correct size. Check the specifications from the maker. It is next to impossible to make over an inletted blank to fit a different rifle.

To begin, remove the barreled action from the old stock, using a screwdriver with the correct blade width. After this has been done, test the fit of the new stock. In most instances, if the stock has been purchased from a reputable maker, you will find that only a bit of snugness here and there prevents the two from fitting together. This is intentional. The barrel channel will be the most noticeable of these areas.

A round inletting rasp is best for working down these areas, although sandpaper around a wooden dowel will do nearly as well if you are careful. A sharp carpenter's chisel will be adequate for shaving down flat surfaces.

Before beginning to cut, however, you must determine just where the tight areas are. A good way of doing this is to mix a spoonful of ordinary vaseline or petroleum jelly with a small part of black oil paint, available in tube form from any hardware store or art shop. Lightly smear the metal areas where wood and metal should go together. Then, if the stock is temporarily fitted to the metal, the areas in need of working down a trifle will show plainly. Shave or sand these down a bit at a time, testing the fit as you go. One critical area in any stock is the recoil lug. This must fit snugly, and be perfectly square in the face. Otherwise the rifle won't shoot accurately.

When the stock is worked down so that all elements fit, it's best to fit the trigger-guard and magazine-floor section first. For this, use a pair of screws to situate that part in line with the receiver. Special ones are available at any large gunsmith shop, but aren't entirely necessary. Two small hardwood dowels, one for each guard screw, and of the same diameter, may be screwed temporarily into the holes, and will serve to line up the floor plate and action. The dowels may be whittled with a pocketknife. When the floor plate is temporarily in place, the dowels should fit into the holes of the receiver, through the stock.

The action and stock are then fitted together for a final testing. In cases where any alteration of the stock must be made to fit the individual shooter, it should be done at this stage. The barrel channel should be sanded down only to where a slight amount of pressure will remain at the junction of the fore-end and muzzle—say from 3 to 5 pounds. When the stock and barreled action fit, the stock is ready for sanding and finishing.

To sand the stock, start with a medium-grade sandpaper, gradually going to a finer grade as the work progresses, finishing with number 000, or as fine a grade available. Then wet the outside of the stock with a damp cloth or wet sponge, and dry it. You will find that a fuzz appears in the wood's grain. Sand this off with the finest sandpaper. Again wet the stock and dry it, and sand once more. Six such sanding and wettings will suffice for most stocks. At this stage, no more fuzz will appear. The stock is now ready for a finish.

Finishing a Stock

A good, old-time stock finish was ordinary boiled linseed oil, applied sparsely, a few drops at a time and rubbed with the palm of the hand until the oil disappeared. The stock was then allowed to dry for a few days, and the process repeated. After several treatments a walnut stock would take on a deep, smooth finish. This is still a fine way to finish a stock.

Modern finishes, however, will speed the job. One product is Linspeed. This is basically a condensed linseed oil product, but can be applied much more rapidly. Another is Nu-Stock, useful for finishing a new stock or for touching up scratches and mars in an old stock.

The hard plastic finishes which now appear on many of the finest rifles can also be put on by the amateur. These finishes consist of epoxy resin, and are applied to the stock in one or more thin coats with a spray gun. Suspend the stock by two wires ending in hooks which go through the inlet of the wood and hold the stock in midair. Apply the epoxy several feet away, in a very fine spray, being careful not to get enough finish on at a time to cause it to run or sag.

If by mishap you inlet a stock too deeply, don't throw it away. It may be glass-bedded. Glass-bedding consists in gouging out the barrel channel and other areas even further, then applying liquid glass to the channel and allowing it to set solid. Manufacturer's directions will come with the product, and if followed, will save a bungled job of inletting. Many shooters glass-bed a rifle now and again anyway, to make a more perfect fit and make it shoot better.

Cleaning Guns in an Emergency

Once in a great while it happens to even the most careful shooter—he stumbles and pokes his gun muzzle into snow, mud, or dirt. The muzzle is clogged and must be cleaned before the gun can be safely fired. To fire a gun with an obstructed barrel is like bellying up to a buzz saw.

With a shotgun, the problem is usually solved without much trouble. The bore is large enough to permit entry of a stick or reed. The foreign material can be poked loose, then removed by blowing through the tube and wiping the inside with a handkerchief on a stick. Usually not over 6 inches will be plugged—it would take a mighty fall to plug a shotgun barrel more.

Cleaning out foreign material from a rifle barrel is much harder, but can be done with nothing more than what the average hunter wears. I learned this the hard way, years ago, when my wife stumbled and fell while on a deer hunt and plugged the end of her Model 99 Savage.

The first thing to do is to unload the weapon. Next, clean out most of the obstruction with a thin stick that has a tiny knot or hook at the end. A stalk of heavy beargrass, a small reed, or any stick that will fit into the muzzle without binding will accomplish this much. If no such stick can be found, the tough root of a plant, or the stem of a dried weed or flower, can often be used. Lacking these, a stick can be whittled out of some kind of available wood.

The next step is to remove one of your shoe- or bootlaces. Into one end of a lace, cut a slit approximately ½ inch long. This slit should not be too close to the end or it may tear. Then cut a patch of cloth from a handkerchief, coat lining, or shirttail which is slightly smaller than the patch you usually use with a cleaning rod. (The patch for a .30-caliber rifle is 2½ inches square.) Insert the patch in the slit.

If the rifle has a bolt action, remove the bolt and insert the lace from the receiver end, and work it through to the muzzle. Then grasp the lace above the muzzle and pull the patch through the barrel. Two or three patches will clean out the dirt, and the rifle will be safe to fire again.

A length of fishing line will serve the same purpose as a bootlace. Fold the line back upon itself at one end for 3 inches, then take the doubled end and tie a double overhand knot. Make two turns about, instead of one. The finished knot will then hang vertically with the patch, not at an angle which would make it bind. A half-inch loop formed in this way will hold the cloth patch. A nail tied to the other end helps in dropping the line through the barrel.

Sighting-In a Rifle

Until a rifle is sighted-in, it is just a combination of wood and metal that won't hit where is is aimed. Most rifles coming from the factory are roughly sighted-in. To shoot with precision, a rifle must be sighted-in by the man who is going to shoot it. No one else can do it correctly.

The first thing to determine is the range at which the sight setting will coincide with the target. No rifle will shoot perfectly "flat" for any distance, and there are only two points in the bullet's arc of trajectory which will precisely coincide with the point of aim. Consequently, it is necessary to sight-in for an average range, then hold over or under for longer or shorter ranges. A .22 rimfire rifle may be sighted-in for 100 yards, but for shorter ranges it will be necessary to hold lower, and for longer ranges, higher. A good sighting-in range for a big-same rifle of the .30/06, .270, .308, or .284 class is 200 yards.

To sight-in for such a range with a rifle and cartridge of this power, it is necessary to have a target and a target butt of some kind to stop the bullet's flight, and some form of table or bench on which to hold the rifle firmly. A steep hillside, or a target butt (which will be described later), will safely stop the bullets. A bench-rest, or a table on which a rolled tent has been placed, or a rolled tent used with the shooter in the prone position, will all suffice to hold the rifle firmly.

With a bolt-action rifle, remove the bolt, set the rifle in a firm position and aim through the bore of the barrel so that the target appears in the exact center of the aperture. To maintain a steady position, hold the rifle butt with both hands.

With the target in the center of the bore, and the rifle held firmly, shift the eye until you can see through the sights. If the line of the sights, or the reticle of the scope, appears to be also on the target, the rifle is then sighted-in closely enough to get "on the paper," or somewhere near the bull's-eye.

If the line of the sights and bore do not seem to coincide, you must make adjustments in the sights until they do. To move the point of impact to the *right* with open sights, the rear sight must be moved to the *right*. To lift the impact *upward*, the rear sight must be

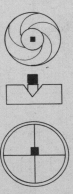

Sighting-in a rifle, showing bull's-eye centered in bore (top), and correct sight picture for open sights and scope crosshairs.

shifted *up*. In short, the rear sight must be moved in the direction you want the shots to go.

When sighting-in with a scope, or when bore sighting, if the reticle appears too far to the left in a trial shot, the rifle is currently shooting to the right and the windage dial must be adjusted "left." A crosshair or post which appears to be low when the target is centered in the bore indicates that the rifle shoots high. The elevation adjustment must then be made in the direction of "low." Some variation in this rule will be found, owing to barrel whip and other peculiarities of the individual rifle, but basically the generality will hold.

With the bore and scope adjusted so that both are on the target, fire a few trial shots, holding the rifle rigidly. A couple of shots will indicate about where the rifle is hitting. Then make the necessary windage and elevation adjustments.

For example, if a .30/06 cartridge using a 180-grain bullet of standard factory velocity hits exactly on the mark at 200 yards, that bullet in its flight will be about 2.4 inches high at 100 yards, on at 200 yards, 9 inches low at 300 yards, and 27 inches low at 500 yards.

It will be obvious that if a bullet starts from the muzzle below a rifle's line of sight, it must cross the line of sight, rise above it midway, then drop down to the exact line of sight in order to be "on" at, say, 200 yards. This means that a bullet will cross the line of sight at two places—one near the rifle, the other far out. With rifle cartridges of the 2,700-3,000 foot-second class, such as the .30/06, .284, etc., this first crossing occurs about 25 yards in front of the muzzle, when an average scope sight is used.

Because of this fact, and since some rifles of the lever-action or automatic class do not permit removing the bolt for bore sighting, you can get a rifle initially on target simply by shooting until it sights-in exactly at 25 yards.

A second way of sighting-in a hunting rifle is first to decide what outside range will be the limit at which you would ever shoot at game—say 350 yards. Then sighted-in the rifle as just described. For shooting at intermediate ranges, simply hold the sights lower in relation to where you want to hit. With some rifles, this may be as much as 5 inches. The first method, for this reason, is best for the average shooter.

Simple Shooting Bench

A shooting bench is a convenient aid for sighting-in rifles. The simple bench illustrated was made in a couple of hours from scrap material left over from a new building.

Four round fence posts approximately 4 inches in diameter and 30 inches long are used for the legs. These form the four corners of the bench: the front legs are 19 inches apart, the rear legs 44 inches apart. Nail two sets of 1-by-8-inch rails to the legs. To the ends of the bench nail bottom rails. The front top rail is a 2-by-4, 40 inches long, nailed flush with the post tops with its ends extended evenly beyond each of the posts. This supports the tabletop at the forward end. About 36 inches behind this 2-by-4, nail another 2-by-4, 42 inches long, in two corresponding slots cut in the tops of the two side rails. At this stage, the framework resembled a four-sided pigpen.

The top, made from 1-by-10 lumber, is 42 inches wide and 40 inches long, with the exception of the right-hand board which is a 1-by-12, 52 inches long, and tapered to serve as an elbow rest. Nail these top

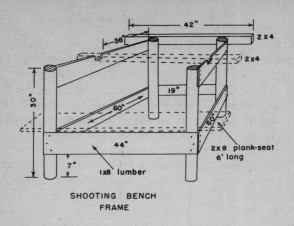

SHOOTING BENCH
FRAME

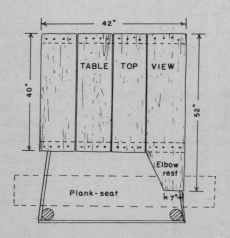

boards to the 2-by-4 crossbars with 8d common nails.
Place a 2-by-8 plank, 6 feet long, across the two side
rails, just inside the rear bottom rail, to make a seat. Do
not nail the plank to the rails so that it can be adjusted
to fit the individual shooter.

Fore-End Rest

An essential accessory for the shooting bench is a rest for the fore-end of the rifle. It should be solid to prevent barrel wobble and adjustable to fit individual shooters or different types of rifles. A good rest can be made from scraps of lumber and concrete.

First make a rectangular box of 1-inch lumber whose inside dimensions are 13½ inches long, 5 inches wide, and 6½ inches deep. In nailing the box together, allow the nail ends to protrude so they can be pulled with a hammer. Place an empty coffee can, with the lid on, in the box with half its diameter protruding. Hold it in place with a couple of nails at each side.

Mix a small batch of concrete in the ratio of 1 part Portland cement to 5 parts sand-and-gravel, and add water to a sticky thickness. Pour this mixture into the box and carefully poke it down around the can so that no air spaces remain. Fill the box level with the top.

After the concrete has dried for two or three days, disassemble the box by pulling out the nails and remove the can. Rub off the raw edges of concrete with a

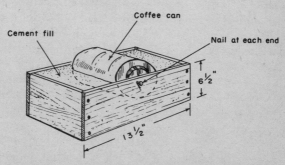

Fore-end rest made by pouring cement into a wood box. Coffee can affixed in the center creates concavity for sandbags.

stick. You now have a block of cement with a rounded depression in which to place sandbags. When sighting-in, the fore-end of the rifle is rested on the bags.

Sandbags

While getting the sand-and-gravel for the rest, it's wise to buy a few shovelfuls of pure plastering sand for making sandbags to put in the crescent-shaped opening. You can make a sandbag from an odd piece of canvas 12 inches long by 6 inches wide. Fold it over and run a seam along the three open sides, leaving a 2-inch opening at one end. Pour the sand through this hole (after turning the bag wrong side out) and sew up the opening. With two bags you can make adjustments in the height of the cement rest to accommodate any shooter or rifle.

Backstop

The best possible backstop for a shooting or sighting-in range is a large mound cut away to leave a vertical face. If targets are placed against this face, bullets will be stopped safely. But for those who don't have mounds in their backyards, a safe shooting backstop can be made of 2-by-12-inch planking and 4-by-4-inch posts.

First cut sixteen 4-foot lengths of planking. Cut four 4-foot 4-by-4s for corner posts. Nail four planks to a pair of posts to make a panel. When you have made two panels, stand them up and nail on the remaining planks. The result is a square box, open at both ends.

Place the box at the end of the shooting range and fill with sand or dirt, tamping as you shovel. Not even a bullet from .300 Magnum rifle will penetrate such a

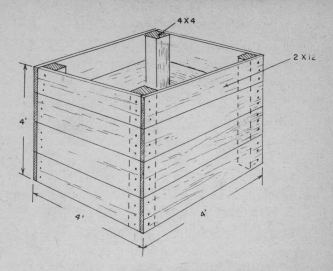

Wooden backstop for sighting-in range.

backstop. When the two middle planks behind the target become damaged after long use, pry them off with a wrecking bar and nail on new ones. Red pine planking, rough sawed, is the best wood for this backstop.

Sighting-In Targets

The best target for sighting-in a rifle is simply a sheet of yellow typing paper with a 2½-inch square of black paper (black film backing or construction paper) thumbtacked to its center. This simple target has many advantages. The best possible visual contrast is the combination of black on yellow, and thus the target is easier to see than other. The square bull's-eye gives more lineal distance in the area where the scope's crosshairs are superimposed on the target, than would a

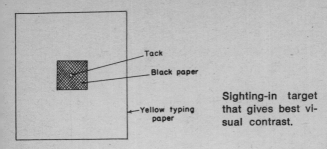

Tack

Black paper

Yellow typing paper

Sighting-in target that gives best visual contrast.

round bull's-eye. It is easier to "fit" the reticle on the target's edge. This is true for a post or crosshair, and for a hold at six o'clock or center.

Shotgun Targets

Many shooters want to test their scatterguns on a target to learn what the pattern might be. In the past, this has been done mainly by aiming and firing at a 30-inch circle on paper at 40 yards. Gun manufacturers normally test their tubes and chokes on the basis of what percentage of the pellets will hit within a 30-inch circle at that range.

A far better target for the average shotgun shooter is a drawing of a game bird or waterfowl in flight. Such a test will give a far better indication of what is actually happening if the shooter casually walks up to within 40 yards of the target and fires quickly, as though field shooting.

Of course, the matter of lead must be disregarded in such a test, but it will plainly show any shooter where he is shooting in relation to where he *thinks* he is shooting. It will also show what pattern his shotgun will give. And it will additionally indicate if alterations in his shotgun should be made, to help him to "hit where he looks." Poor stock fit often adversely affects aim.

Bird targets are easy to sketch. Use black crayon, charcoal, or other plainly visible media. The targets should be drawn approximately life size. As examples, a life-sized quail, in flying position, will average around 9 inches. A mallard will be about 22 inches, a Canadian Honker nearly 36 inches, including wingspread. Newsprint is a good paper to use for these targets. It may be obtained from any big newspaper publisher in the form of roll ends left over from the presses.

After shooting, scribe a 30-inch circle around the thickest portion of the shot pattern. Mark the holes made by the tiny pellets with the eraser of an ordinary pencil which has been inked on a pad. From such a pattern, you can see in which direction you miss your target and what kind of a pattern your gun throws. If the 30-inch circle encloses the bird, you are shooting well.

Shotgun target for testing the pattern of shot.

30" circle at 40 yds.

Shortening and Crowning a Rifle Barrel

Occasionally you may want to shorten one of your rifles. You may want to remodel a long-barreled military rifle, or repair a damaged muzzle, or modify a rifle for mountain hunting. This should be done before finishing the stock or sighting-in.

To shorten the barrel, clamp the rifle firmly in a vise (with padded jaws, as mentioned before), and cut off the extra length from the muzzle end with an ordinary hacksaw. A sharp blade will eliminate the need for extensive finishing-up work.

Even so, the cut made by such a saw will be rough, and in most instances slightly off "square." Before the rifle will again shoot accurately, the muzzle must be squared off at a true right angle to the bore, and the edges of the lands must be smoothed.

The easiest way to square off the muzzle is with a large, flat bastard file. The longer the file, the less it will wobble as you work. One who has done a lot of metalwork with a file will be able to file squarely across the muzzle without tilting the file.

To do a perfect job of flattening the muzzle, it is best to use some kind of guide. The simplest is a square of 1-inch board with a hole bored in its center exactly the diameter of the muzzle. The muzzle is shoved through the hole until the end of the barrel just perceptibly protrudes from the other side. If the board does not fit tightly around the muzzle, it may be wedged with a sliver of wood from the rear side of the board until it is tight.

Next, clamp the gun barrel in the vise with the muzzle up (most people can file better with a lateral stroke). With the muzzle in this position, file gently across the board. The file will touch only the metal if

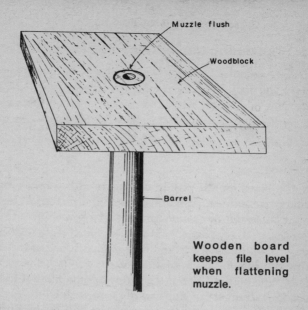

Muzzle flush

Woodblock

Barrel

Wooden board keeps file level when flattening muzzle.

care is used, but if bits of wood are filed off it won't matter. The file will cross the muzzle squarely. The board won't allow it to tip. The result will be a barrel end which is perfectly flat and at true right angles to the axis of the bore. Unless this is accomplished, one or more of the barrel lands will extend imperceptibly farther than the others, and this will impair the rifle's accuracy.

The remaining job is to crown the muzzle. In remodeling a military rifle, or cutting down a barrel on an average rifle, it is not necessary to finish the muzzle with the type of crown found on factory rifles or expensive custom rifles. An adequate crown can be made by slightly countersinking the bore at the muzzle and smoothing it down evenly all around.

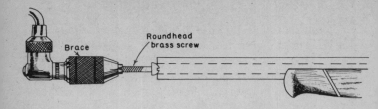

Crowning the muzzle with roundhead brass screw in brace.

The simplest way to do this is with a brace and a large, roundheaded brass screw. Other materials necessary are a bit of ground emery and a few drops of olive oil.

Clamp the sharp end of the brass screw in the jaws of the brace, put a mixture of the ground emery and olive oil on the head of the screw and, holding it lightly against the bore at the muzzle, turn it slowly. This will smooth and slightly countersink the end of the bore so that the land ends are precisely the same all the way around.

If a deeper countersink is desired, a sharp-angled countersink bit may be used first, before grinding with the brass screw-head. The bit should be held precisely in line with the axis of the bore, touched only lightly to the muzzle, and turned evenly. This will cut the lands to the desired depth, after which the screw and emery will impart the finishing smoothness.

Complete the job of crowning by smoothing down the sharp outside edge of the muzzle. If you are handy with a file, simply touch this edge lightly with the tool, and with an even turning stroke, touch away the sharp edge.

If you have a lathe, or other means of revolving the entire rifle barrel, you can do an even smoother job.

As the barrel turns, hold the file lightly against the outside edge of the muzzle at a 45-degree angle.

After crowning the muzzle in this way, a touch of cold-blue, applied according to directions on the cut portions of the muzzle, will finish the job. Or the entire barrel may be reblued in a regular bluing tank.

Thwarting Condensation

The rusting of the metal on guns comes from the action of oxygen on water, particularly salt water. Anyone familiar with guns knows that water or snow must be removed within a matter of hours or rust pits will occur in the metal. This is ordinarily accomplished by cleaning the gun all over after moisture has touched it, and then coating the metal parts with a light film of good gun grease or oil.

A more treacherous form of water is moisture resulting from condensation. Condensation comes from rapid changes in temperature. Moisture condenses upon the cold metal, which violently cools it and turns it to water. This means that guns brought out of the cold into warm tents or cabins will have moisture condensed upon the metal parts. A scope sight used in cold weather will fog up when exposed to warm air.

The way to beat condensation is simply to avoid subjecting guns to quick changes of temperature. This is often difficult since hunters normally hunt in cold weather and bring their guns inside a warm tent or cabin at the end of the day. But when bringing a gun into a warm tent or cabin, you can wrap it in a hunting coat or parka. Then place the wrapped gun on a bunk temporarily, where it will gradually adjust to the room's temperature. The insulation of the coat will permit the room's heat to get to the gun gradually, preventing a sudden change in temperature.

A good way to wrap a gun in a coat is to poke the barrel into a sleeve, then wrap the body around all other metal parts so the receiver and scope are covered. Twist the end of the sleeve to shut off heat over the muzzle.

This is the way to prevent camera lenses from fogging. In the Arctic I constantly brought a pair of cameras into a warm hut when outside temperatures averaged around 26 degrees below zero without fogging the lenses. I wrapped both cameras in my down parka before entering the hut and left them that way for an hour or so.

At cold-season hunting camps, some outfitters leave their clients' rifles *outside* the tents during the night. After cleaning them, the hunters store them in a special rack built for the purpose. Both the rack and guns are covered for the night with a canvas tarp. No condensation occurs, since no quick changes of temperature take place.

When a horseback hunter carries his rifle in a saddle scabbard, the heat of the horse's body will cause condensation on the rifle whether the weather is warm or cold. A rifle carried for several hours, during the normal fall hunting season, will show condensation on the metal parts.

Moreover, the salt from the horse's perspiration will penetrate the best scabbard leather and rapidly rust the weapon. A cardinal rule in horseback hunting is never to leave a rifle in a scabbard overnight. Always clean the rifle, coat it with a thin film of oil or grease inside and out, dry out the sweat-soaked scabbard each night inside the tent or cabin, and do not replace the rifle in the scabbard until the next morning. One of the best commercial products for protecting a gun against condensation is the product Rig.

Finally, condensation can ruin a gun's metal, or the stock finish if the weapon is stored in an airtight case. It's always smart to loosen the zipper a few inches, or leave a solid case unlatched, during home storage.

Storing Guns at Camp

One place to store guns at camp is in an outside rack, as mentioned before. To make such a rack, find a pole about 3 to 5 inches in diameter which is long enough to stretch between two trees. Drive a number of 8d nails, at a slight upward angle, 4 inches apart, into the pole, then nail or lash it between the two trees at a 30-inch height. The length of the pole depends on the number of guns to be stored. Then smooth the ground beneath the rack and lay one side of a canvas tarp beneath the pole. The butts of the rifles are placed upon this part of the tarp and the balance is folded over the muzzles and back behind the pole.

A gun rack of this type should be placed where there is no hunter or horse traffic, and where rain or snow will not fall on it—such as under the branches of a big spruce tree near the tents. The weight of the canvas will prevent wind from blowing it off the guns.

When keeping guns inside a tent, don't put them on a sleeping bag or bunk that is being used. Condensation will inevitably form on the underside of the gun from heat remaining in the bag or in the ground beneath it.

One of the best ways to store a rifle inside a tent for the night is to hang it by the sling from a nail driven into the rear upright of a wall tent. The rifle may be hung either with the muzzle up or down. In a big wall tent which has a long wooden pole runing along the top of each side wall, a fine place to hang a rifle is from a nail driven into one of these. But be sure the muzzle does not touch the tent fabric. Rain on the fabric will inevitably seep off and into the gun barrel. Also, the gun should never be hung so that any part of it touches the ground—it will accumulate moisture. For the same reason, rifles should not be stacked in a corner of a tent with muzzles against the canvas.

When storing any gun at camp, the most important rule of all is to unload that gun before entering the camp, keeping the muzzle pointed *downward* while it is being unloaded.

Rack for storing guns in camp. Tarp folds over the muzzles to protect them from rain.

Once in Wyoming I got off my cot and walked outside to see if a late hunter had bagged his elk. The hunter was dutifully unloading his rifle, but his muzzle was not pointed downward. Somewhere along about cartridge number three his finger got the trigger. He plowed a hole through the tent, the cot where I'd been five seconds before, and into a supply of groceries stored under the cot. The bullet would have hit mè dead-center.

Reloading Ammunition

Among the reasons for reloading one's own ammunition are saving money, developing a better load for a certain gun, and experiencing the thrill of shooting a better target or taking the annual buck with a cartridge of your own making.

The equipment needed for handloading is minimal: a press, dies, loading block, powder scales, funnel, powder, bullets, and primers. The once-fired cases from factory ammunition are fine for reloading the same caliber. Complete reloading outfits cost from $50 up.

Before attempting to reload your own ammunition, study a good manual on the subject and carefully follow the instructions. Good manuals include *Lyman's Reloader's Handbook, Hornady Handbook of Cartridge Reloading, Speer Manual for Reloading Ammunition,* and Ackley's *Handbook for Shooters and Reloaders.* Besides detailed instructions, all these books include loading data for most popular cartridges. These are tested, safe loadings. *Never exceed the loads listed in these manuals, and always stay just a trifle below maximum loads until experienced in making up handloads.*

Handloading is divided into several simple steps: inspection of cases; case lubrication; resizing; decapping; priming; checking primed cases for fit, charging with powder; and bullet seating.

Inspection means to scrutinize all empty cases for flaws, and to throw away any case that is split, dented, or otherwise not perfect. Such cases are not safe to reload.

Lubricate the empty cases so they will enter and emerge from the constricting dies easily. Do this either by rolling them on a pad of heavy towel which has been oiled with a good commercial lubricant, or simply by wiping them all over with a cloth which has been lightly lubricated. Care should be used to see that no lubricant gets into the open mouth of the case.

Resize lubricated cases, either full length or only at the neck. New cases, unless factory resized, and empty cases fired in another gun, should be resized their full-lengths to give them perfect fit. A once-fired case may be only neck-sized, if it is to be shot in the same chamber.

To resize, set the empty case into the shell holder of the tool and actuate the lever. This pushes the case upward into the die, which resizes it to standard dimensions after the case has been expanded through previous firing. Also, as the case goes into the die, the central punch pushes out the old fired primer. Then, as the case is started from the die, place a primer in the tool's primer arm. This is placed under the empty primer pocket. As the case is further withdrawn, the live primer pushes into the primer pocket, and the primer arm is then flipped out of the way.

The sized and primed case is then totally withdrawn from the die. In doing this, an elliptical "button," which is integral with the central punch and on the top end, comes out the neck of the case. This button resizes the inside of the case neck as it emerges, so that the bullet will seat snugly.

With the case now sized and primed, inspect it again, and see if it will fit the intended chamber. Neck sizing, incidentally, is done by backing off the die in the tool for about half a turn, so that the die doesn't touch the case's shoulder.

To charge the sized cases, select a suitable type of powder, and weigh each individual charge on a powder scale which will weigh charges to one-tenth of a grain. The type of powder and number of grains is obtained from the loading data in the manual. I repeat: *maximum charges of powder should never be used by the beginning reloader*. Loads a grain or two under maximum will deliver almost as much velocity, and are safe to use. It's wise to remember that you're dealing with pressures up to 50,000 pounds per square inch or more; and that a difference of only a fraction of a grain over maximum will cause such pressures to skyrocket. The person who innocently decides to use a maximum load ("—surely a few grains more will make a better, faster load") is flirting with certain disaster.

Each powder charge, after being weighed, is funneled into an empty, primed case which is stood upright in the loading block.

When all the cases have been filled with powder, the bullets are seated. This is done with a second die, a part of the set, called a bullet seater. The seater is placed in the tool, the charged case is set into the shell holder, and a suitable bullet of the type, caliber, and weight recommended in the loading data is held on top of the case mouth. The tool's lever is again actuated, allowing the bullet and case to go into the die, which seats the bullet firmly inside the case neck.

In seating bullets, a good rule to follow is to seat any rifle bullet to approximately the depth of one bullet diameter. A .30-caliber bullet normally should be seated about .3 inch into the case neck.

With all bullets seated, the completed reloads are then taken from the loading block, wiped free of all oil, packed in cartridge cases, and labeled.

A good loading block, by the way, can be made with just a brace and bit and a 2- by 6-inch plank 18 inches long. Bore the plank in the pattern of a grid, with holes about 1 inch apart. A ⅜-inch bit is appropriate for .30-caliber cases, and all holes are bored nearly through—just to where the bit's point begins to protrude. Labeling should indicate the date and data of the load. For example: "May 5th, 1970. Speer 100-grain softpoint bullets. 47 grains #4831 powder. Winchester #120 primers. .257 Roberts caliber. Seating depth .25 inch. Velocity 3,000 fs. Good antelope load."

Shells for handguns and shotguns are reloaded similarly, but with differences in dies and, with shotguns, somewhat altered steps in the process. Every good reloading tool will include detailed instructions for its operation.

Reloading for rifles will cut the cost about 50 percent. Shotgun reloading will cut the cost approximately 40 percent. To further reduce the cost, it is wise, as long as available supplies last, to use military surplus powders, available in bulk, which for hunting purposes are comparable to the commercial powders. Such powders currently cost a dollar per pound and under. Two of the finest are military powders #4895 and #4831.

When the beginning reloader reaches the point where he wants to reload faster, powder measures and turret-head reloading tools, as well as other specialized equipment, are all available. But the basic equipment described above will get him started.

Light Rifle Sling

Commercial rifle slings are usually too heavy for hunting, especially in mountain country. They are patterned after military slings designed for target shooting.

The hunting sling has two uses—to carry the rifle and to provide a quick, solid hold when shooting. The hasty sling is used in hunting, as against the arm-loop hold in target shooting. The hasty sling is assumed by thrusting the left elbow (for right-handed shooters) downward through the space between rifle and sling at the bottom of the rifle, and placing the left hand

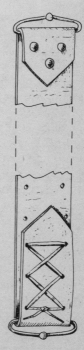

Light rifle sling made from latigo leather, riveted at fore-end swivel and laced at butt-stock swivel.

around the forward portion of the sling and gripping the fore-end. Moving the hand backward produces tension and holds the sling tight. In that way, the sling helps hold the hunting rifle better in the off-hand, sitting, kneeling, and prone positions. The sling must be of proper length to do this.

Only a very light strap is needed to make a hasty sling. A length of latigo leather (meant for cinching a saddle) 1-inch width and 3¼ feet long is suitable. Or a length of 1-inch tanned buckskin may be used. A regular latigo strap may be cut to width if it's too wide.

To attach the front end of the sling to the rifle, fold it into the swivel from the outside, and fold it back 2 inches upon itself. Punch three holes of suitable size, in triangular form, through both sections of the strap. Rivet the strap together with three black rivets, the two-part type available at the 5-and-10.

If you can't stand the thought of metal rivets in a sling, you can lace the strap to itself with a length of leather thong or shoelace.

The lower end of the sling similarly goes through the lower swivel, then folds back over itself. Instead of riveting this end, lace it to fit your arm length. Punch a foot-long series of holes in the leather, approximately ³⁄₁₆ inch from the edges and about 1½ inches apart.

Try the fit of the sling with a partner hoding the lower end in place. A trial lacing will indicate whether the length is correct. It's wise to make the length about one hole too short at first since the leather will stretch somewhat.

I have a strap sling that was placed on a 7 mm rifle in 1941, and it still fits me today. That little rifle has taken deer, antelope, black bear, coyotes, and even elk over much of the western part of this continent.

The Rifle Scabbard

The stiff carbine-length military scabbards that are still available at surplus stores are unsuitable for sporting rifles. If you cannot find a scabbard to fit your rifle, have one custom made.

A scabbard for a scoped rifle should cover the rifle at least as far as the scope. Better ones cover the entire stock and fasten with some kind of flap or snap fastener at the butt end so that they may be undone quickly. The leather for a good scabbard should be stiff, but not exceptionally heavy. Otherwise the scabbard will pull too heavily on one side of the horse, causing galling, or otherwise crippling its back.

One position for a scabbard is on the right side, under the stirrup, pointing forward and down, with the butt high at the back of the saddle. When you dismount to shoot, you can grasp the butt over the horse's back as you swing down and to the left. The only trouble with this position is that the rifle may slip from the scabbard when you're riding up a steep hill.

A better way of carrying a scabbard is in the Northwest position. Here the scabbard rides on the horse's left side, beneath the skirt of the stirrup, with the butt forward and the muzzle down. In this position, the bolt is away from the horse, and the stock is easily grasped as you dismount on the left side. Also, when you spot game and neck-rein the horse, you are concealed by your mount as you pull the rifle from the scabbard—often avoiding frightening the game.

I have found that the best way to attach a scabbard to a stock saddle is to use a 2-foot strap with a ⅝-inch buckle at one end and holes at the other. To each of the straps encircling the front and rear of the scabbard—the scabbard loops—place a ¾-inch harness

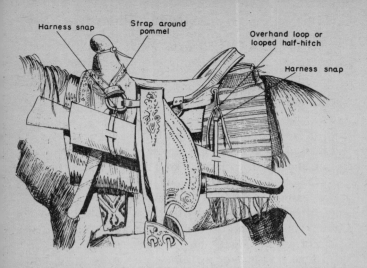

Harness snap   Strap around pommel   Overhand loop or looped half-hitch   Harness snap

Method of attaching rifle scabbard to saddle in Northwest position.

snap, obtainable at any hardware store. These snaps remain threaded into the loops at all times.

In use, the first strap and buckle is tied around the pommel of the saddle below the horn, through the opening in the saddle tree, and down around the left bulge. Twice around is fine; then buckle down the strap tightly. This strap remains on the saddle for the entire trip. To put the scabbard on the saddle, the snap on the front scabbard loop is simply snapped through this strap around the pommel. The rear snap is then attached to a saddlestring, at proper height, at the rear of the saddle. To attach this snap, the leather saddlestring is looped with one half-hitch through the metal snap, and the loop pulled tight. There is little rifle weight on the rear loop, and such a string, pulled taut, will hold.

To remove the entire scabbard at night, or when

leaving the horse to stalk game on foot, pull the rear saddlestring from its loop and unsnap the front buckle—a matter of five seconds. This type of attachment is also good in case of a fall.

The most important thing to remember about using a saddle scabbard is *never* to carry a chamber-loaded rifle. If there isn't time to chamber a cartridge after dismounting, there won't be time for a decent shot at game anyway.

Simple Duck and Goose Decoys

American Indians made simple waterfowl decoys of bunches of grass tied together to resemble sitting or feeding birds. To make them more natural, they often smeared mud on the bundles, giving them a mottled appearance similar to the female birds. After a bird was killed, it was set among the decoys with its head propped up in a natural pose. Today, waterfowl are more sophisticated and more natural-looking decoys are needed to bring them into range.

Simple decoys are easy to make. A stake silhouette decoy, made of ¼-inch plywood, can be painted to simulate either ducks or geese. Find a suitable picture of a live bird, either feeding or resting—the larger, the better. Such pictures can be found in most outdoor magazines or on calenders. Trace the bird on a piece of thin typing paper. Next mark a grid over the traced picture. For example, say that the picture is of a standing Canadian goose about 3 inches high. A good grid size would be about ¼-inch. To make the grid, rule off parallel lines with a pencil, horizontally and vertically, over the tracing. These may be numbered with letters in one direction, with numbers in another for later reference.

If you want the decoy to be 18 inches high, or about natural size, mark off a larger grid on the sheet of plywood from which the decoy is to be cut. The squares of this grid are proportionately larger. In this instance, the ratio of picture to decoy is 1 to 6, so each square will be 1½ inches.

Into each of the large squares on the plywood, draw the same line as in the corresponding square on the tracing. The result is a larger outline of the bird, in true proportions. Cut this out of the plywood sheet with a keyhole saw.

To paint the decoy, get some white paint and a tube of oil-black from a hardware store. The largest part of the goose will be a dull gray. Mix the color and paint the entire silhouette. Next paint the white areas with white paint, the black patches with black paint. With about three or four color mixtures, and some blending of the colors, plus a bit of dark daubing to resemble individual feathers, you can make a natural-looking goose. If you are more artistic, you can paint drakes and birds with more color.

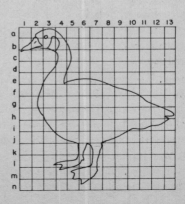

Draw decoy on paper ruled with a grid to aid in transferring the pattern to plywood.

There are two good ways to make stakes to hold the decoys in the water. One is to nail a length of wooden lath to the body, letting it extend 15 inches so that it resembles the leg of a bird, and sharpen the end. The other method is to use a wire stake. Bend a length of #10 galvanized wire into a short right angle at the top. Poke it through a small hole drilled through the decoy body about 5 inches from the bottom. To hold the wire in place, drive a small staple over the wire through the decoy. Or secure the wire stake with fine wire, wound through two pin-sized holes on either side of the stake. If a lath stake is used, it should be nailed to the body before painting, and then painted the color of a leg or as a part of the decoy.

Head decoys can be made from plywood and painted in the same way. Set the pointed lath stake at a slight angle off vertical to represent the bird's neck. Head decoys are very useful for attracting birds that feed in grain stubble that covers their bodies.

Estimating Bird Flocks

Have you ever wondered how many ducks or geese were passing overhead during migration time? There is a knack to estimating bird flocks with a fair degree of accuracy. As the flock flies by, quickly count a group of ten birds at one edge of the mass and make a mental picture of the space they occupy. Then superimpose that block on the rest of the flock and determine its number in multiples of ten. Even though individual birds change their position in a flock as they fly, this system is remarkably accurate. Just count the number of blocks and multiply by ten.

When counting geese flying in a wedge formation, there is time to simplify the blocking further. Count

Estimate bird flocks by counting group of ten and visualizing number of blocks in the entire flock.

ten birds, then get an image of a line of fifty birds, and superimpose this image on the entire migration.

You can estimate the number of elk, deer, or antelope in a herd with the same system . . . taking a mental picture of ten animals and counting the number of blocks.

Blinds

Blinds are often necessary to allow a hunter to conceal himself from close-ranging birds. Such blinds take many forms, but they all should be made to blend with their surroundings by using natural materials. If such materials are not available, the blind should be constructed in advance to permit the game to become accustomed to it.

A good blind for waterfowl can be made from driftwood. Simply arrange a pile of driftwood along a river course where ducks pass so you can get inside it and huddle down. The less you alter the original pile, the better. Wear camouflage clothing to match the surroundings. With such a blind you will be indetectable to the wisest waterfowl.

Similar blinds can be made of down timber by crisscrossing lodgepole pines along deer trails and game runways. In the desert, blinds for hunting antelope can be made of sagebrush casually bunched into a covering at the edge of an alfalfa field where game habitually comes at daylight. The hunter gets there early and waits inside. I once used such a sagebrush blind to take closeup photos of "booming" sagegrouse. Some came within 20 feet

During late fall along snowbound rivers, snow blinds are excellent for hunting geese and ducks. Snowdrifts at the water's edge, hollowed out to contain the hunter (who should wear white), provide good camouflage.

In the West, in bighorn sheep country, there are still the remains of rock cairns which the Indians built to hunt the wily animals. These cairns were made by piling up talus into a 3-foot "box" adjacent to a sheep trail. One or more hunters would wait, huddled inside a cairn, while others frightened bands of sheep from below. When the animals filed by, the hunters shot with bows and arrows. We once used this type of blind at the edge of a lake in lava country and took limits of ducks which skirted by, unable to detect us huddled inside the pile of rocks.

Camouflage clothing can be made easily and is one of the most effective blinds. In snow country, a bedsheet with a hole cut in the middle, worn like a poncho, is good camouflage. A large white handkerchief tied over your cap completes the deception. Another method is to use a 10-foot length of white cloth, 3 feet wide, with a hole cut in the exact center. Place the cloth over your head and tie the gaps at each side loosely together with cloth tapes sewed to the edges. This costume allows the arms enough freedom of movement for shooting.

I have found the best white costume for snow hunting to be a pair of white coveralls such as painters use, plus a white-covered hunting cap. If bought a size too large, such coveralls will conceal the hip boots ordinarily needed for waterfowl hunting. The garment should be bleach-washed in advance to take out the yellowish tint.

Camouflage garments are readily obtainable in mottled shades to match autumn foliage. Several yards of similar camouflage cloth can be carried along, worn as needed, or built into small hutlike blinds over brush framework. This kind of blind is paricularly useful for varmint calling in desert areas where the location of the blind must be periodically changed.

A fine blind for goose and duck shooting in stubblefields is chicken wire stuffed with straw. Sit down and cover yourself with the "blanket"; you will resemble a small haystack. This blanket is also useful for pit-shooting in stubblefields. After digging a pit, cover the fresh earth with straw, lie down in the pit, and cover yourself with the straw blanket.

Perhaps the strangest blind of all was described to me recently by a Canadian friend who has learned how to outwit Canadian honkers in prairie stubblefields. He learned from long observation that his cattle and horses didn't frighten wild geese. So he cut from plywood a life-sized silhouette of a horse, painted one side, and attached a couple of hand-holds. When a flock of geese lands in his fields, he takes his shotgun and horse and wanders casually towards the resting birds. By taking only a step or so at a time, and artfully keeping the horse's painted side toward the geese, he can get with shooting range.

Hanging Heavy Deer

If you bag a heavy deer, and want to hang it to cool before getting it to camp, here are three practical methods:

Even if the deer weighs 300 pounds, you can hang it with three poles and a length of rope. The poles should be slender, about 7 or 8 feet long, trimmed of branches, and sharpened at the large ends. Lay the poles on the ground, with their tips together just above the dead deer's antlers and their butts extending outward like the spokes of a wheel. Lash the tips together, somewhat loosely so they won't bind later, and tie the end of the rope to the deer's antlers or head. Leave a foot or more of slack between the antlers and the poles.

Stand over the deer's head and lift his neck and head off the ground, raising the pole tripod enough so that the sharpened ends stick slightly into the dirt. Then push each pole, in succession, inward and upward, a little at a time. The tripod will gradually become erect, and the deer will hang off the ground to drain.

The second method of hanging a huge buck (or elk quarters) also requires a tripod. Before you erect it, tie a long, slender pole just under the lashing, about 3

Tripod used to lift deer into hanging position.

feet from its large end. Tie a short nylon rope to this end of the pole, a longer piece to the other end, and drive a stake where the pole meets the ground.

Erect the tripod to full height so the sharpened ends of the three poles set firmly into the ground. Lift the buck's head as high as possible with one hand, at the same time bringing down the short end of the pole by the rope tied to its end with the other hand, and tie a half hitch around the antlers. Then pull on the hitch, holding what is gained, and bring the buck's head a couple of feet off the ground. Tie solidly. All that remains is to pull on the free rope at the pole's end, bring it down and tie it to the stake.

Tripod and pole for hanging a deer.

The third method is practical if a deer is killed on a hillside with trees. After cleaning the deer, drag it to a tree and leave it on the uphill side. Lop off all branches on the uphill side, then tie the buck's antlers or head as high as possible off the ground. Next, cut off the branches on the downhill side so the carcass can swing freely. Shift the deer's body around the tree to the downhill side. Depending on the size of the deer, and the steepness of the hill, the carcass will swing freely. If it doesn't, tie a rope to one or both of the hind feet, pull it away from the hill, and tie the end to a bush or a stake.

Deer tied on uphill side of tree, allowed to swing to downhill side after branches have been cut.

Simple Game Hoist

A lone hunter can hang a heavy deer or elk quarters with nothing more than two small pulleys and a length of nylon cord.

The pulleys should be light, since they must be backpacked on the hunt. Two awning pulleys, about 2 inches long, of light metal, are strong enough to lift weights of up to 200 pounds and over. You also need a 30- to 50-foot length of 150-pound-test nylon rope.

To make the hoist, attach a yard of rope to the eye loop of each pulley. One rope will be tied to the deer's

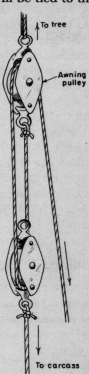

How to use two small pulleys as a game hoist.

antlers, the other to a tree or tripod. Thread the remaining length through the pulleys, as shown in the illustration.

The leverage gained by this simple arrangement is 2 to 1. If you weigh 200 pounds, you therefore can lift a deer of well over 300 pounds. If you want to lift heavier loads, use pulleys with double blocks.

Buttonholing a Deer

If you are hunting alone on horseback and kill a large mule deer, here is an easy way to bring it back to camp. After cleaning the deer, make an incision about 2 inches long just inside the meat of the belly at the point of the sternum. Then, using the game hoist previously described, lift the deer off the ground and lead the horse under it. Grab the deer by the legs and swing it across the saddle. Insert the saddle horn in the incision. Tie the antlers back so they don't gouge the horse, and tie the legs on either side to the cinch rings. In tying the legs, it's best to cut slits just above the knee joints through which the ropes can be passed. Tie the ropes to the front of the cinch ring, otherwise the lashing tends to tip the ring into the horse and injure it. When leading the horse back to camp, avoid traveling through heavy brush that will catch the loaded animal on either side.

Packing Elk Quarters

The proper way to pack elk quarters out of the hills is to use a packhorse and packsaddle. However, if you are ever caught with an elk down and only a bareback horse or mule, you can pack half an elk with only a length of rope.

When dressing the elk, cut the carcass into halves instead of quarters—that is, leave the front and rear quarters together. Cut the meat and bone of all quarters through the dividing lines between them, but cut the skin only between the front and rear halves. This cut is made behind the third rib of the carcass. The result will be a set of front quarters and a set of rear quarters, with a skin hinge running the length of the halves.

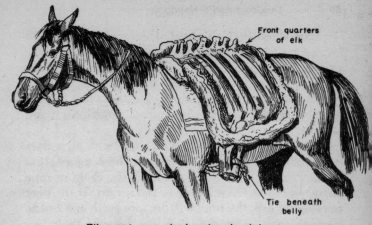

Elk quarters packed on bareback horse.

Slip the halves onto the horse, hair side down, so that the right side of the elk rides on the left side of the horse. Cut slits above the knee joints on either side and tie the legs together at these points, running the rope under the horse's belly. Wrap a coat or shirt around the rope so it won't rub the horse.

Skidding and Travois

Besides packing, there are two ways of getting deer-sized game to camp. The carcass can either be skidded along the ground by two hunters or hauled by horse on an Indian-style travois.

The best way for two hunters to skid a big deer is with the aid of a sapling about 4 feet long and 2 to 3 inches in diameter. Cut holes in the deer's forelegs through the skin and between tendon and bone, just above the knee joints. Shove the sapling through these holes as the deer lies on its back. Tie the head, or antlers, between the forelegs against the sapling.

Each hunter takes an end of the sapling, lifts it till the deer's shoulders clear the ground, and walks away with the deer. Only the rear part at the hip bones will touch, and though this may rub off some hair, no meat will be damaged. I have helped drag deer like this for distances up to four miles without damage, on ground partially covered with snow.

If a horse is available, with harness only, a deer can be similarly dragged on snow without injury. It is dragged head forward. Always hitch the chain or rope to the deer's underjaw, never to the antlers. If the deer is antler-hitched, the tines will dig into earth and brush. Antelope can't be dragged this way because their hair will be rubbed off.

The Indians used a travois for skidding game to camp behind a horse. You can make a simple travois of two slender poles about 12 to 15 feet long. Tie the small end of each pole to the saddle rings above the cinch, allowing a short length to protrude so it won't

Using a sapling to skid a deer out of the woods.

pull out. Next lash a number of green saplings across the poles, far enough behind the horse to clear its hoofs, forming a simple platform. The deer is placed on this platform and tied down. When the horse is led toward camp, the butt ends of the two poles drag on the ground like runners. Use a martingale, or breast strap, with a stock saddle to prevent the saddle from being pulled back by the dragging poles.

Scalding Chicken or Grouse

Most hunters simply skin a grouse by cutting the skin at one leg, and tearing it off in strips until all skin is removed. The only cuts necessary are at the legs, the wingtips and front of the wings, and around the neck.

However, you may wish to pluck some species of upland birds, or exceptionally fat birds. The easiest way to do this is first to scald the bird. The feathers then come out with little effort.

Place the bird head first in a small bucket. In this position the hot water will go down against the base of the feathers. Boil enough water to cover the bird, and allow the water to cool for a couple of minutes. Then pour it over the bird, holding the legs and moving the bird in the bucket to get complete coverage. Swish the bird around until it is completely scalded. About two minutes are necessary for an average grouse, but a tough old bird takes longer. The right "scald" is at that point where all feathers become loosened, but before the bird becomes partially cooked. A freshly killed bird scalds easiest.

With the bird scalded, hold it by its feet and pull off the feathers in small tufts. (Pull the feathers toward the bird's head.) Singe off remaining pinfeathers with a lighted roll of newspaper.

Plucking Waterfowl with Paraffin

In a recent letter, Salmon River outfitter Don Smith told me how to pluck a duck or goose with paraffin:

"Get a 5-gallon can and put in 4 gallons of water. Bring the water to a boil, then shave in a couple of

Water and paraffin

5 gal. can

Waterfowl immersed in can of water and paraffin to remove feathers.

pounds of paraffin wax. When it melts, push the goose down through the paraffin. Hold it under like scalding a chicken. Then pull the goose slowly up through the hot paraffin. Let the goose drain over the can. Then head for the back door as fast as you can go, dripping only small amounts of paraffin on the kitchen floor. While the goose is cooling on the back porch, see if you can get the paraffin off the kitchen floor. After the goose cools, pull off the wax scab, and it is ready for the pot."

That's the basic technique, but here are a few suggestions.

It's easier to pull off bunches of the heaviest feathers before immersing the fowl into the water and paraffin. This leaves less area to pluck, and allows the melted wax to penetrate to the base of the feathers. Hold the duck or goose by the head or neck—there's less danger of scalding the hand. For a single bird, or a few small ducks, the proportion of water and wax may be retained but in smaller quantity—say, half as much solution. Finally, in warm weather (which is rare in duck season), the wax will cool quicker if the fowl is first dunked into a pail of cold water. The remaining pinfeathers can be removed by singeing with a lighted roll of newspaper.

Skinning Big Game for Trophies

If you want to make a wall trophy of a big-game animal you have killed, the worst mistake you can make is to rush up and stick the animal in the throat and cut off its head behind the ears. Good taxidermists can repair such field mistakes to some extent, but the trophy later will show "ropes" of bulging skin where these cuts have been made.

For deer, antelope, sheep, goat, caribou, elk, and moose, only two cuts in the skin are necessary to remove the cape in the field. The antlers or horns are later cut out as a "plate."

The first cut begins well back upon the animal's withers, and proceeds in a straight line up the center of the neck until a point between the ears is reached. From there a short cut is made to the base of each antler or horn, forming a Y in the neck cut.

The second cut begins at the withers, and proceeds

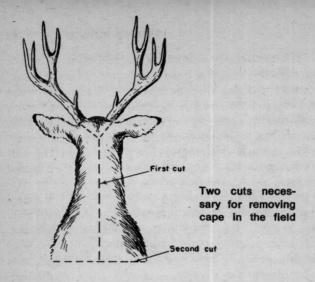

First cut

Two cuts neces-
sary for removing
cape in the field

Second cut

down through the middle of one shoulder, around in
front of that shoulder, well down below the brisket,
and similarly up the opposite shoulder until the starting point is reached. In making this second cut, it is
well to remember that "too much cape skin is just
right." The taxidermist can cut off surplus skin far easier than he can locate skin to match a cape which is too
short.

From these two skin cuts, the neck and shoulders
of the animal can be skinned out all the way to the
medulla, or occipital protuberance. At this joint where
head joins neck, the animal's head is then cut and
twisted off, leaving the head inside the skin. In cool
weather, or if the taxidermist can be reached within a
few days, the head and cape will keep if it is salted well
over the exposed flesh surfaces and inside the eye, ear,
and nostril orbits.

If a taxidermist cannot be reached soon, it is necessary to skin out the head completely. This is done, without further cutting, by reversing the skin over the head as it is skinned away. Special care should be given to see that the ears are cut off very close to the skull, and that the lips and eyelids are not cut in any way. The caped skin should then be salted all over. The antler plate is now cut from the skull, as described in the next article.

Where even further delay is encountered, the ears must be skinned, or the skin covering them will slip. The ears are skinned by folding them wrong side out, and cutting delicately between the outside covering and the cartilage. After an ear is partly skinned, it is easier to finish if a mildly pointed stick is pushed up inside the folded ear. This brings the thin, delicate junction between ear skin and cartilage into position for separating it with the pointed blade. The ear must be skinned to its very tip.

It is only necessary to skin the outer side of each ear, leaving the cartilage integral with the inner side. A good salting of the skinned portion will keep it from spoiling. Many taxidermists leave the inside of the ears unskinned, and place the ear form between the outer ear skin and the cartilage.

Game animals which are not intended for head and shoulder mounts, but which are to be used as rugs or full skins, are field skinned in a different way. Here the entire skin is taken off with three cuts.

Place the animal on its back, and make the first cut lengthwise along the abdomen from anal vent to throat. At this point, you may either continue the cut up through the center of the chin or angle off to the corner of the mouth. With bear hides, the finishing cut to the mouth is preferable, since the seam that sews it up will show less.

The second cut begins at one hind foot, runs across to the base of the tail (just inside the thin skin of the inner hind leg), and across to the opposite hind foot.

The third cut goes across the chest in a straight line from one front foot to the opposite front foot.

The four feet are either left integral with the skin, or the skin is girdled around each foot, leaving the feet

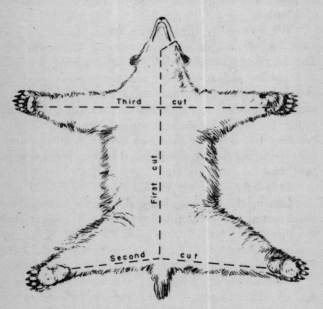

Three cuts for skinning an animal for entire hide.

with the carcass. With bear and other furred animals, the feet are normally left integral with the skin. When skinning a bear, first cut around the four foot-pads, but not the toepads, and then skin out each individual foot. Depending on the coolness of the weather, you can skin out all bones of the feet without making further cuts in the hide. This applies also to the animal's head. All flesh areas are then heavily salted.

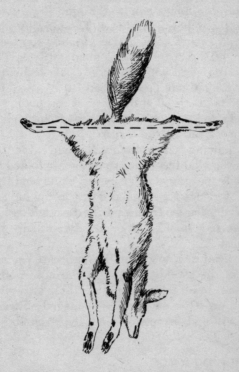

Single cut for skinning small, furred animals.

Skinning Furred Animals

Smaller furred animals such as foxes, coyotes, and wolves often are used as full-hide trophies, but as cased hides to be hung on a wall instead of flat, rug-type mounts. The animal must be "cased" during field skinning.

To case a furred animal, make only one cut in the skin, from one hind foot across to the anal vent (just inside the thin, inner hair of the hind leg), and then across to the opposite hind foot. The hind feet are not girdled but cut off at the ankles, leaving the feet with the hide and the bones to be skinned out later. The tail is also left integral with the hide. (The technique for skinning the tail will be described later.) It is best not to cut the tail bone off at the base, at this point, since it is far easier to remove the entire bone from the tail skin if the bone is left on the carcass.

All skinning is done from this single cut in the skin between the hind feet. The skin is simply folded downward while the animal is suspended by its hind legs.

The forelegs are skinned down to the ankles, the bones of the leg severed, and the feet left inside the hide. The feet may be skinned later, usually by the taxidermist.

The head is skinned over the nose, care being taken not to cut the eyelids or lips. At the nose point, the nostrils are cut off where the gristly nose area joins the bony septum. This leaves the undamaged nostrils with the hide. All flesh areas are then heavily salted.

Skinning Birds

To prepare a game bird for mounting, the body must be removed from the skin, and the skin salted so it will keep until it reaches the taxidermist.

It is necessary to make two cuts in the skin. One goes from the anal vent up along the center of the belly line as far as the point of the breastbone. The other, shorter cut is made from the medulla of the bird down the center line at the back of the neck for a distance of 2 inches (for pheasants). These cuts are in heavily feathered areas and the subsequent seams necessary for sewing up the hide will not be visible in the mount.

The entire body of the bird is removed through these two cuts. The neck is cut, through the neck incision, and worked down into the body cavity. The legs are disjointed at the large end of the drumsticks, the meat pared away from the bones down to the junction of skin and lower legs, and the thigh bones left inside the bird's skin.

By carefully working the skin away from the body at the back and at the wing bases, the entire body can be removed through the belly incision. (After the wings are cut off at their bases.) All meat is removed from the skin, which is then heavily salted. Care should be taken to insure getting salt into the base of the skull, and the leg and wing areas. If a camp cooler is available, the skin may be wrapped in paper and kept in the cooler until the taxidermist can be reached.

How to Make an Indian Hide Frame

The Indians used a simple frame for stretching and fleshing hides. The frame was made just larger than the outside dimensions of the hide. The hide was placed inside and stitched to the frame with thong. With the hide roughly in place, the thong was tightened evenly, stretching the hide taut but not out of proportion. The frame was then stood on a slant in the shade. In desert regions, where wood was not available, the Indians pegged their hides to the ground.

The modern hunter could well use a hide frame for stretching his animal skins. Too often, he simply tosses his fresh deerskin over a pole and forgets it. The

Frame used by Indians for stretching and fleshing hides.

raw skin tends to curl at the edges and shrink. But if a deerskin is stitched to a frame soon after the kill, it will dry out quickly and remain in good condition until it is used for making wearing apparel or other articles.

Cutting Out the Antler Plate

Antlers or horns that are to be mounted on a wall plaque must be solidly attached to a section of the skull. This section is called the antler plate.

On some mounts, the skin of the animal is left on the antler plate; on others it is removed and the plate covered with velvet or other material. If you want to retain the skin, it must be cut away before cutting the skull.

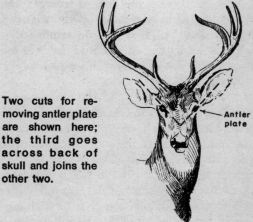

Two cuts for removing antler plate are shown here; the third goes across back of skull and joins the other two.

Antler plate

The skull is cut with three separate incisions. One goes squarely across the back just above the medulla. The other two are made on each side so they join the first cut at the base of the skull, go down the face *through* the bony eye orbits, and join midway down the bone of the nose. Don't make the side cuts above the eye orbits. This will ruin the skull plate since the remaining section will not have the rigidity necessary for holding both antlers. Often an entire plate is broken by cutting in this fashion.

If the animal has been packed into camp, a saw is the best tool for this job. But for cutting out an antler plate where the animal is dropped, a good ax will do. Hold the animal's head solidly, and keep cutting on the same lines until the bone is severed. Scrape away the remaining brain parts and take the antler plate to a taxidermist.

Skinning a Canine's Tail

In field dressing a coyote, fox, or wolf for mounting, the tail bone should be removed. Otherwise the tail will look unnatural. The best time to remove the tail bone is while skinning the animal, and the best tool to use is a length of willow or alder split lengthwise exactly through the center.

After making the cut in the skin from one hind foot to the opposite foot, the carcass should be skinned out for a few inches each way around the anus, the base of the tail, and the rump area. This makes room for working out the tail bone.

At this point, the skin of the tail is folded back over the tail itself and skinned all around with the sharp point of a small blade, much as in skinning out an ear. The folded-under fur of the tail will tend to bind it to the tail bone; and it is only possible to skin the tail, as it is folded over itself, for a few inches.

Next take the split stick and, with the boot toe held between the base of the tail and the skinned hide, place the halves on either side of the skinned tail, with their flat sides inwards. Grasp the sticks on either side of the tail bone, hold the toe firmly against the root of the tail, and pull, stripping the remaining skin from the tail bone. The tail bone will still be attached at its base, and the skin of the tail be left integral with the body skin. Finally, work salt into the tail opening.

Where willow branches are not available, a pair of pliers from a motor vehicle toolbox is a good substitute. Hold the tips of the jaws in one hand, the handles in the other, and pull hard against the folded skin at the base of the tail.

Keeping Meat in Hot Weather

Most big-game hunting seasons are timed for fall and cool weather, partly so meat can be kept without spoiling until it can be taken home. However, you will occasionally bag game during a period of hot weather, and unless you know how to take care of it, especially during the first critical hour, it will spoil.

Spoiled meat can be caused by animal heat, blowflies, or predators. To thwart animal heat, the game must be quickly dressed and the carcass cooled. This may be done either by quartering and hanging the carcass so that air circulates all around it, hastening the cooling process, or by using a substitute which will accomplish the same purpose. This applies to the larger game animals such as elk, moose, and caribou. Deer-sized game may be cooled without quartering, unless the weather is extremely warm.

A light game hoist, mentioned before, is suitable for hanging a carcass. Often, though, a large game animal will be killed away from timber, in an area where there are no suitable trees for hanging the quarters. In such instances, the meat may be quickly cooled if a can of black pepper and a brushpile are available.

First, dress the animal, being careful not to allow any intestinal fluid or urine to touch the meat, as they will taint it. Next, quarter the carcass. This hastens cooling and makes it easier to handle.

With the animal dressed, the next important step is to smear fresh blood over every part of the exposed flesh, being careful to coat those areas where skin meets flesh. If the animal's fresh blood cannot be saved for this purpose, in a small puddle, then it's best to smear all available flesh areas while the liquid blood is in the chest cavity, after dressing and before the final quartering. The meat areas remaining from the quartering may then be smeared with liquid blood before it coagulates.

Smearing the flesh areas with blood will cause a glaze, or seal, over the flesh, which will protect it against blowflies. In order for blowflies to lay their eggs, and for the eggs to turn to maggots and ruin the meat, the insects must have both warmth and moisture. The blood glaze will occur quickly, especially in hot sunlight, forming a seal against the blowflies and cooling the flesh.

Parts of the meat that cannot be covered with blood can be sealed by sprinkling the moist flesh areas heavily with black pepper. This will dry up flesh rapidly. A half-pound can is sufficient for four elk quarters. Black pepper on the flesh surfaces will not harm the flavor of the meat.

Next comes some real effort. From available foliage make a huge brushpile, large enough to accommodate all four quarters of the carcass without piling them on top of each other. More important, it must be bulky enough so that, when compressed by the quarters, it will stand about 18 inches high. This will allow the air to circulate completely around the quarters, accomplishing the same purpose as hanging the quarters by allowing animal heat to escape from all surfaces. For it is animal heat, not weather, which spoils game meat.

Finally, with the quarters glazed with blood, dried with pepper, and resting on the brushpile, place a light covering of loose twigs on the top side of the meat so that magpies, eagles, and other predators cannot peck at the flesh. Coyotes, incidentally, won't touch it for at least twenty-four hours, unless storm washes out the man scent.

Deer-sized game can be cooled on a brushpile and left unquartered if it can be handled by the lone hunter. For a large deer killed in warm weather, if the head is not to be saved for a trophy, it is best just to open up the body by cutting through the sternum at the rib cage and split the backbone so that the entire carcass can be laid flat with the hide side down.

After the carcass has been placed to cool on the brushpile, hurry to camp for help and get it back and hang it. The meat will be set up by then, and can be moved without damage.

By-Products of the Hunt

Tanned animal hides can be used as throws for the back of a divan or as wall decorations. They can be made into vests, coats, fringed shirts, or gloves. Numerous leatherworking firms which advertise in outdoor magazines will make garments from deer, elk, and moose skins.

Various uses can be found for the feet of game animals. A pair of ram or antelope feet mounted on a plaque makes a fine rack for holding a rifle on the wall. Save the forefeet of the animal by cutting them off at the knees and take them to a taxidermist.

The feet of large game animals can be made into attractive ash trays. Elephant feet make unusual ash-tray stands for a trophy room; those of smaller animals are suitable for desk ash trays.

The forefeet of grizzly and brown bears can be

transformed into bookends. Skin the legs from the knee joints. The feet can be left for the taxidermist. To skin the feet yourself, simply make a cut down the back of the foreleg and completely around the pad.

Sections of deer or elk antlers make fine handles for hunting knives. Several knife makers now furnish blades and tangs for the do-it-yourselfer who wants to make his own hunting knife. A thin slice of elk antler with a small hole bored in one side serves as a rustic key ring. Thread the key chain through the hole, and burn or paint your name and address in the center.

Elk teeth, which are the only pure ivory found in North America, are suitable for tie claps. Persuade a jeweler to set a pair into a gold cap and you'll have a handsome souvenir of the hunt. Likewise, the "eyes" of elk teeth can be turned into a pair of earrings.

Ivory teeth are found only at the back of the elk's upper jaw—the teeth on the lower jaw are all calcium. Many hunters fail to remove these teeth from the skull because they don't know how or believe that special tools are required. Actually the only tools you need are your hunting knife and a couple of sticks.

First, with the point of the knife cut between the tooth and the jawbone completely around the tooth. These cuts should be made as deeply as possible, but without prying with the blade (it is apt to snap off). Just insert the tip of the blade at the outside of the tooth, then strike the butt of the knife's handle with the palm of the hand. Dig between tooth and jaw to a depth of about a half inch around each tooth.

Next, find two sticks, a heavy one to use as a hammer and a smaller one for a tool.

The tool should be about a foot long and 1½ inches in diameter. A dry spruce limb broken from a nearby tree is excellent—tough but brittle—and will snap off squarely. (A wooden tool is preferable to a pair of pliers, since the metal often scars the enamel.) The "hammer" can be a heavy piece of wood, or even a rock, weighing a pound or more.

Hold the tool firmly against the front part of the ivory tooth—that is, the edge nearest the animal's nose—and hit it sharply with the hammer. One sharp blow will dislodge the tooth without damaging it. Whittle the remaining flesh off the root area with a pocketknife, and the tooth is ready to be made into an ornament.

The brown "eye" of the tooth is the valuable part, and its depth depends on the age and condition of the elk. But to deepen the brown of the eye, and impart a deep brownish luster to the tooth, all that is necessary is to place the tooth into the canvas pocket of a pair of jeans, add a spoonful of unused coffee grounds, and keep it there for a couple of weeks. This will impart a beautiful brown polish to the ivory.

Bear Fat For Boots

The hunter who bags a bear, either black or grizzly, has the makings of a fine boot conditioner—the fat that coats the bruin during the autumn hunting season. Bear fat will not only make leather boots far softer than many boot greases, but will to some degree waterproof the boots.

Perhaps the best time to apply bear fat to boots is just after the animal has been killed and skinned. Simply rub the boots on the fat remaining on the carcass or the skin.

To keep bear fat for future use, it is necessary to render the fat and store it in a cool place. Chunks of fat can be rendered in a skillet or even a tin can at camp, and the melted oil allowed to set in a can or jar. Do not add salt as it will damage leather. At home it can be kept in cold storage, or in an outside building during winter months. It sets up as a pure white lard. I know several mountain men who use the lard from a fat, young black bear for cooking.

How Indians Made Arrowheads

Arrowheads were usually made of flint or obsidian, rocks that chip or flake easily when worked with an abrasive tool. Indian camps were often located in areas where there was an abundance of these rocks.

To make an arrowhead from a large piece of obsidian, a small piece was broken off by striking it a glancing, oblique blow with a rock. If the obsidian was hit at the center, it would split or shatter. Obsidian tends to "shear" when struck in this way, and a thin slice usually comes off the main piece. The slice may be broken further with judicious strokes of the rock. Of course, when metal became available to the Indians, they used it for breaking obsidian.

When a thin, elliptical piece of obsidian was broken off, it was chipped into an arrowhead with a tine of deer antler. The tine was squared at the point, and after a little use became rough enough to catch the edge of the obsidian. The arrowhead was folded in a piece of buckskin to prevent injuring the hand and to enable the worker to hold the piece solidly on his knee.

By working on one side of the edge, then on the opposite side, the arrowhead could be shaped and thinned as desired. Notches were chipped at the base of the head for binding it to the shaft.

Arrowheads can be made today in the same way, but a better tool than a deer antler is a 16d spike im-

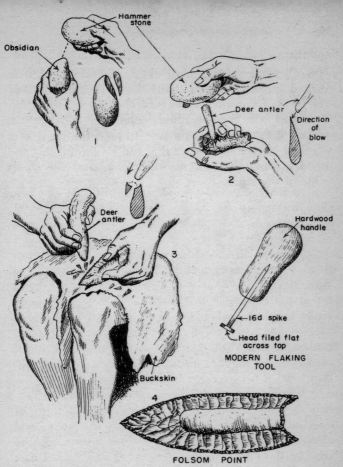

FOLSOM POINT

Indian chipped small piece from obsidian with stone hammer (1). With small length of deer antler, he chipped large flakes, forming the basic shape of the arrowhead (2). He completed the job with a large antler tool (the larger the antler, the finer the flake), putting a sharp edge on the arrowhead by fine flaking (3). Finished Folsom point (4) shows fine flaking along edges, large flakes on total surface. Groove to fit shaft was knocked out with blow on either side.

bedded in a piece of hardwood. Cut off the point of the spike, leaving a 3½-inch shank, and insert it in a hole drilled in a small piece of hardwood. File the surface of the head of the spike so that it is flat. After a little use, the head will become rough enough to bite well in chipping the obsidian. Be sure to hold the head in a piece of leather so it won't slip, and be careful that the hand holding the tool doesn't slip against the sharp edge of the stone.

PART 2

Fishing How-To

Emergency Fishing Kit

A wilderness fishing kit for emergencies must be portable enough to be carried on your person, otherwise you're apt to leave it at home. A simple kit consisting of four items will catch fish in the wilderness.

1. Dozen fly hooks.
2. Ten-yard roll of monofilament fishing line.
3. Small bobbin of silk thread.
4. Six paper clips.

The twelve hooks should be of assorted sizes, ranging from #12 to #4. They should be of the wet-fly type, and of good quality. The majority of hooks should be of average size, #6, #8, #10.

To the sophisticated angler, casting into his home stream with expensive equipment, this may not seem to be much of a fishing outfit, but I have used these items to catch fish in wilderness country.

Our remaining wilderness areas are remote areas, and the fish there are unused to anglers and generally easy to catch. Also, in most North American wilderness areas grayling will be found, and this species is particularly easy to catch. I have caught numerous grayling, up to 16 inches long, using only emergency tackle.

The monofilament can either be attached to the end of a springy branch or used as a handline. A better rod can be made by bending the paper clips into guides and lashing them to the branch with the silk thread, as explained in a later article.

If worms or other bait cannot be found, the thread is also used to tie emergency flies. Full instructions for tying flies in the wilderness are given in the next article.

Half a dozen wooden matches, paraffin dipped to be waterproof, should be included to start a fire for cooking the fish.

The entire kit will fit into a plastic envelope, which should be sealed tightly with plastic tape. If it is sewed into the pocket of your fishing jacket, you'll be sure not to leave it behind when you venture into remote areas.

Tying Emergency Flies

I once proved to a group of skeptics that it was possible to catch fish with emergency flies tied with materials found on the spot. We were on Tanada Lake, in Alaska. The first fly was made with some hair cut from my chest and a wormlike strip of blue wool from my shirttail. The second was tied from a tuft of my wife's hair and a tiny strip of silver foil from the wrapping of a roll of film. The third fly was made from a single bald-eagle feather found along the shore.

These flies were all tied without a fly vise, bobbin, pliers, head varnish, wax, or any equipment save the bare hooks. The hooks were held in the hand while the flies were tied.

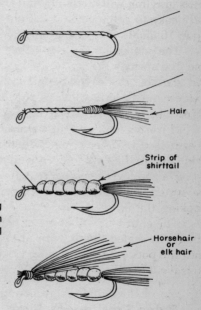

Four steps in tying emergency fly with strip of shirttail and animal hair.

The first two flies were tied in this manner: The thread was tied into the hook's eye and wound spirally down to the shank where it was half-hitched. A few hair fibers were tied on for a tail, and held by two more half-hitches. The shirttail "body" (or foil strip) was tied at the rear and wound on to the head of the hook.

The thread was similarly wound on spirally to the same point where it was secured by more half-hitches. Lastly, the hairs used as a streamer were wound on at the head. Four or five half-hitches just behind the hook's eye completed the job.

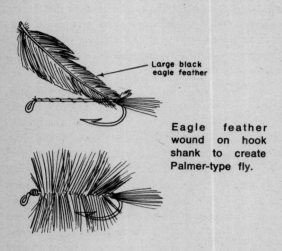

Large black
eagle feather

Eagle   feather
wound   on   hook
shank   to   create
Palmer-type fly.

The third fly was made using only a hook, thread, and the black eagle feather. Several fibers from the quill end of the feather were bound on for a tail. The tip was then tied at the shank, and wound spirally up the length of the hook, Palmer fashion, and secured at the head. A "head" was wrapped on with several turns of the thread, and several half-hitches finished the job.

With these three flies, four people, taking turns with a fly rod, caught over a dozen grayling weighing up to 1½ pounds. Every fly caught fish, and not one of the crude patterns was worn out.

Tying Flies at Camp

If you have more equipment and materials, you can of course tie better flies. Remember that fish will take flies that attract but do not resemble natural insects. This is especially true of backcountry fish, unused to contact with fishermen.

A pair of pliers, held by your partner, will serve as a fly vise. Lacking pliers, you can sharpen the point of a stick and cut a slit in the tip in which the hook's point is held.

Fly tails can be made of horsehair, squirrel hair, hemp fibers, or yarn from a sweater. Material for fly bodies includes strips of cloth or yarn, hair of a muskrat, squirrel, badger, deer, elk, moose, bear, or pet dog. Even human hair is usable. A rubber band wound spirally in several layers along the shank makes an effective fly body. Strands of burlap from a potato sack make one of the most natural-looking fly bodies imaginable. Grouse, ptarmigan, or sage-hen feathers, bunched together and wound on in the shape of an insect body, are all useful. The main thing in dressing bodies on flies is to make them somewhat elongated, elliptical, and the size of insect bodies.

Hackle is meant to simulate the insect's legs. If feathers are available, one can be wound on at the head. But when no feathers are available, the best thing to do is wind on a streamer. Streamers can be made from bundles of animal hair or from feathers from the shoulder area of large upland birds. If you can find waterfowl feathers, or even the primary feathers of magpies or crows, you have good material for streamers.

A third type of emergency fly—a nymph—can be made of skimpy materials; for example, a bunch of belly hair from a muskrat. Hold a small bunch of hairs between thumb and forefinger and bind them to the shank with spiral turns of thread. Leave a few hairs sticking out at both front and back to resemble tail and feelers.

A hardback nymph can be tied of the same material, with the addition of a small bunch of hair from a squirrel tail, elk, deer, or horse. Tie on the hairs before wrapping on the body so they protrude an inch behind the hook. After tying on the body hair double all but a few of the tail hairs over the nymph's back and tie down at the head. The few hairs sticking out in front simulate the feelers.

Painting Metal Lures

For some reason, fish will strike a lure of one color on one day but will shun it on another. I have found this to be true of cutthroat trout on the Snake River. One day they'll hit a plain brass wobbler, the next day they won't. But if I painted a pair of black eyes on the wobbler they'll hit it. Sometimes a pair of red eyes, or a red stripe, makes them hit.

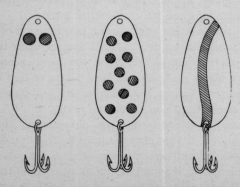

Suggested patterns for painting metal lures.

To add these color variations to lures, I keep a few bottles of fingernail polish in my tackle box. The best colors are red, black, and orange. With these colors I have often changed an unproductive lure into a "taker."

Some of the designs I've found to be effective are a pair of eyes, a stippling of black dots, or a single wavering red stripe running the length of the lure. If the experiment proves unsuccessful, it's easy to scrape off the polish with a knife and try again.

Emergency Landing Net

If you damage your landing net while on an extended fishing trip, or even forget it at home, it's possible to make one from cord or old fishing line. Use the original frame if it's available; otherwise make a new one by bending a long, slender willow into a loop and tying it in place. The loop formed may not be symmetrical, but this won't detract from the utility of the net.

Next cut a number of 6-foot lengths of cord. Double each length at the center and attach it to the loop, as shown in the drawing. These double lengths should be spaced about 2 inches apart.

To weave the cords into a net, tie each of the adjacent cords of a pair, about 2 inches from the frame, with an overhand knot. After you have completed one row of knots there should be a series of half diamonds around the frame. To finish, continue tying the adjacent cords until you reach the ends.

As the tying progresses downward, the lengths forming the diamonds are minutely shortened, tapering the net. When the cords are used up, or when the desired length is reached, tie them together at the bottom. When only a portion of an original net is dam-

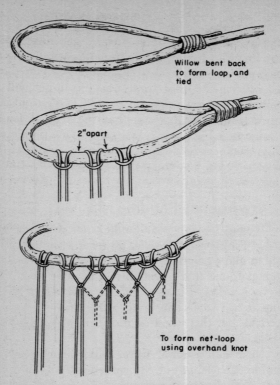

Willow bent back
to form loop, and
tied

2" apart

To form net-loop
using overhand knot

Improvising a landing net from a willow and string.

aged, new cords should be tied around the loop only at
that section. The cords are then tied to the ends of the
original net.

Tying Tapered Leaders

The advent of nylon monofilament has made it
possible to tie your own tapered leaders. You can use
spools of monofilament specially made for leaders, or

lengths of old spinning lines. One of the most useful leaders for trout fishing tapers from an average diameter of 8-pound test down to 3-pound test. This 6-foot leader will handle large trout, and the tippet will accommodate flies down to a #12. The average trout angler can't handle much more than 7½ feet of leader, especially with big trout in fast water. One problem in landing fish in heavy water with a long leader is that the knot joining leader and line will usually run up through the tip guide during the landing process and stick.

To tie this leader, use four tests of nylon monofilament: 8 pound, 6 pound, 4 pound, and 3 pound. In choosing this material, pay as much atten-

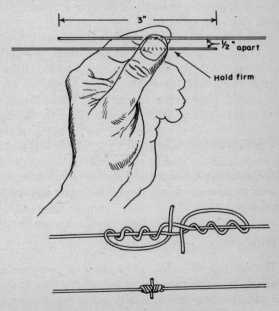

Blood knot for tying tapered leader.

tion to the diameter of the material as to the listed strength. In many cases, 8-pound-test material will be the same diameter as 6-pound test. The basic idea in any tapered leader is to create an extension of the tapered line itself, down to a fine tippet which will allow the line and leader to cast the fly smoothly.

Cut a length 20 inches long of each of the four grades of monofilament. Start with the length of 8-pound test and join it to the length of 6-pound test with the blood, or barrel, knot. To tie this knot, lay the two strands of material side by side, a half-inch apart and overlapping about 3 inches. Next, with the thumb and forefinger of the left hand, grasp the two strands at the center of the overlap and hold them apart. This creates a space between the two strands which is held during the knot tying.

Wind the end of the leader at the left of the fingers three times around the strand next to it and poke it *downward* through the space temporarily held between thumb and forefinger. Then wind the end of leader to the right of the fingers three times around the other length, and poke it *upward* through the space. Finally, pull on both ends of the two lengths of leader until the knot forms and jams tight. The result will be a tiny knot with an end sticking out on opposite sides. These are clipped off just a trifle longer than flush.

With the same knot, tie the 6-pound and 4-pound lengths, and then the 3-pound tippet. After all knots are tied, pull the leader taut for a moment or so to straighten it.

Dropper Loop

A level leader is not as delicate as a tapered leader but it's adequate for fishing bait or large wet flies. Generally a 3-foot level leader is sufficient. Anything longer will be difficult to cast.

When fishing with a level leader, you may want to tie on a dropper to fish a brace of wet flies or a combination of fly and bait. Here are two simple ways to do it:

1. Lay a length of monofilament for the dropper alongside the main leader at its midpoint. About 8-pound test is right, to give the dropper the stiffness needed to keep it from winding around the leader.

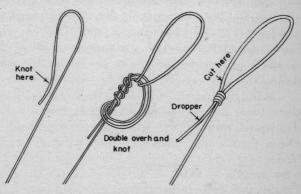

Knot here

Cut here

Dropper

Double overhand knot

Tying a dropper on a level leader. When loop is cut at point shown, it unfolds and becomes dropper.

Grasp the dropper and the leader and tie them together with a double overhand knot. Clip off the surplus end of the dropper, leaving a single length of monofilament running parallel to the leader.

2. At a point about 12 inches from the end, double the leader back upon itself and grasp the two strands halfway up. Tie a double overhand knot at this point. Then clip the leader just below the knot, allowing the loop to unfold into a new length, with the short piece above the knot becoming the dropper.

Splicing a Fly Line

To repair a broken fly line on an extended fishing trip, or to tie on a line of smaller diameter to replace a ruined taper, you must be able to splice. A knot of any type joining the two segments is intolerable since it will not feed through the guides of the fly rod. A simple splice can be made in a a few minutes with a sharp knife and a yard of silk thread.

Lay each end of the two segments to be joined on a flat board. Sharpen the knife to a razor-like edge. One inch from the line's end make a diagonal cut, tapering the line from its full diameter to a point. Take care that the line does not roll while you make this cut as this will spoil the finished splice. Cut the end of the other line in the same way. When the two tapered ends are

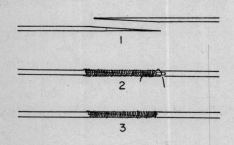

How to splice a fly line.

laid together, the line will retain its original diameter along the length to be spliced.

The splice is made by "whipping" the two ends with the silk thread. Begin by laying a few inches of thread along the splice; then a fraction of an inch above the taper, start to wind the line around the two ends, over the length of thread which has been laid along them. Each turn must be tightly wrapped next to its predecessor, with as much tension as the thread will withstand without breaking. Should the line break, it's best to start over.

When a half inch has been wound, the protruding thread end may be pulled under the winding so that it will not show. Continue winding until a point just beyond the cut ends is reached, as this will tend to smooth the splice. Finish the splice by folding the running end of the thread back over the part which has been wound, so that all further windings will be made upon it. When the winding is finished, carefully pull the free end of the thread, taking up all the remaining thread that has not been used. You'll find that this surplus can all be pulled up between the windings. The extra is cut off close to the winding.

If you have some fly varnish, lacquer, or even fingernail polish at camp, coat the splice with it, work it in with the fingers, coat again, and allow to dry.

When thoroughly dry, the line will cast freely through the guides of the rod. There will be a slight bump in the line, but this won't matter if the trout are biting.

Weighing a Fish with a String

Have you ever caught a big fish and wanted to weigh it on the spot? If you don't have a scale along, you can still determine the weight of your catch with only a piece of string and a stick. The stick should be about 18 inches long and uniform in diameter. Cut a

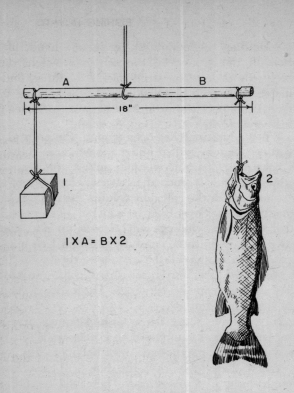

$$1 \times A = B \times 2$$

Crude scale of stick, string, and object of known weight.

small notch about 1 inch from each end. Tie a length of string at each notch. Now tie the end of one string to the fish's jaw. At the end of the other string tie some object of known weight—a boot, a pound of bacon, a can of beans. Tie a third length of string to the middle of the stick with a slip knot. You have now fashioned a crude steelyard with which it is possible to weigh the fish.

Holding the middle string in one hand, lift the stick off the ground so the fish and weight dangle freely. By sliding the string along the stick, find the fulcrum—the point where both objects balance. Mark the fulcrum on the stick and measure the distance from this point to each side string, or notch.

If you don't have a rule or tape, break off a small piece of twig about 1 inch long and use it to measure in "units." The twig need not be exactly an inch in length as long as it is used for all measuring.

The formula for calculating the weight of the fish is: $1 \times A = B \times 2$. As shown in the drawing, $1 =$ weight of object; $2 =$ weight of fish; $A =$ distance from fulcrum to notch on object's side; $B =$ distance from fulcrum to notch on fish's side.

For example, suppose you are using an object that weighs 2 pounds. The distance from the fulcrum to the string supporting the object is 4½ inches, or units. The distance from the fulcrum to the string supporting the fish is 7 inches, or units. Therefore, $2 \times 4\frac{1}{2} = 7 \times B$, or $7B = 9$. (B equals the unknown weight of the fish.) Answer: 1²⁄₇ pounds, or 1 pound, 4⁴⁄₇ ounces.

Measuring a Fish with Your Hand

In early times, the human hand was used as a unit of measurement. During the settlement of the West, the size of a horse was determined by how many "hands high" it was at the withers. The hand is still useful in field measuring fish, antlers, or game.

The average adult hand measures approximately 6 inches wide across the palm—from the fleshy outside at its greatest width below the little finger, to the tip of the thumb. Thus six "hands" would be equivalent to a yard.

To measure smaller distances, lay a grass stalk, leaf, or string across the hand and fold it in the middle. This gives you a 3-inch measuring stick. Fold it again and an inch and a half can be marked off.

With practice, you can measure smaller distances simply by placing the finger of the other hand into the palm. A finger in the center will show 3 inches on either side. This distance, either measured again by the finger into three parts, or just visually marked off, will serve as a gauge for small measurements.

Cleaning Fish

Game fish should be cleaned soon after being caught, otherwise the blood lying against the backbone tends to deteriorate, causing spoilage at this point first. The method of cleaning most small game fish is as follows:

If the fish has noticeable scales, remove these first by holding the fish at the tail and scraping toward the head with a knife or fish scaler. Then remove the entrails by making two cuts. One is a straight incision running from the anal vent almost to the tip of the lower jaw. At the point where this cut terminates well up through the gill coverings, make a second crosswise cut. Just behind the V of the lower jaw tip the outer gill coverings end in a thin membrane, also V shaped, joining the gill coverings to the lower jaw. Push the knife tip through this thin membrane on one side, under the pointed tip of the gill coverings, and out the opposite side—with the edge of the knife toward the head of the fish. Then cut the reamining V-tip of the gill coverings from the jawbone itself. Hold the tip of the gill coverings, which has been severed from the lower jaw, tightly between thumb and forefinger of one hand, and with the other hand grasp the fish by the lower jaw. Now separate the two sections, pulling the gills downward. In most cases, a continuous stripping motion will pull all the gills and entrails from the fish. The only part that tends to stick is that small area where the gills join the back at the fish's neck. Often it is necessary to pinch this area so the gills break free of the backbone.

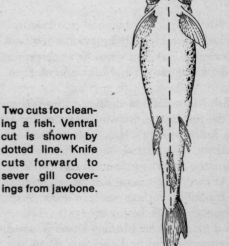

Two cuts for cleaning a fish. Ventral cut is shown by dotted line. Knife cuts forward to sever gill coverings from jawbone.

With the entrails stripped away, remove the layer of blood lying against the fish's spine. Two or three strokes with the thumbnail will usually push this blood out, especially if it's rinsed with water. Then cut a small V across the anus and remove it. The fish is now ready for cooking, with the head and outer gill covering integral with the body.

For larger fish like salmon and steelhead, the procedure is the same except that a bit of cutting is necessary at the point where the top of the gills join the backbone. Usually this will not break away with a pull. Also, to remove the blood at the spine, it is necessary to sever the membrane on either side of the layer of blood, then scrape the blood away. A good tool for doing this with king salmon and large steelhead is a metal teaspoon.

Keeping Fish Cool

Freshly caught fish will deteriorate, soften, and spoil within a matter of hours unless some provision is made for keeping them cool. Cleaning fish soon after they are caught will delay this spoilage somewhat, but more should be done. The best way to prevent spoilage is to place the cleaned fish in an ice cooler. During early spring fishing, a snowbank is a natural ice box. Otherwise cleaned fish can be kept moderately cool by placing them on a layer of grass or moss in the creel. If the grass is kept slightly damp, by periodically sprinkling it with a handful of water, cooling will take place by evaporation.

An 18-inch square of burlap makes a good creel cooler. Wipe the dressed fish free of slime, fold them individually into the burlap, and put them in the creel. sprinkle them every hour or so with a handful of water from the creek.

Besides helping to keep fish cool, burlap has another fine virtue as a creel liner. Much of the odor of dead fish comes from the slime. Burlap will collect most of the slime so that it does not permeate the willows of the creel. The burlap can be washed at home. To further avoid fish odor in a creel, give it heavy coats of varnish each season, on the inside as well as the outside.

If fish must be kept at camp for several hours, in hot weather, burlap can be used to keep fish fresh. Fold the fish separately in the burlap and tie the bundle. Hang it on the shady side of a big tree, near a stream if possible, where a breeze will strike it. Evaporation will keep the fish cool if the burlap is kept lightly moistened.

With the addition of a large tin can, you can make a better cooler. After wrapping and tying the fish in the burlap, punch a very small hole in the center of the can's bottom and thread the can, with the open end up, on the cord. Hang the bundle of fish by the cord, with the can just above. Fill the can with water. The slow seepage of water down the cord through the hole in the can will keep the burlap moistened and cool the fish. If the hole is small enough, the can of water will last for hours.

One last tip: If fish are dressed, wiped dry, wrapped in ordinary newspaper, and buried in moist ground near the water's edge, they will keep cool for hours.

Making Sinkers

Sinkers are used to get a lure down to the proper depth. They are available in great variety, and are so inexpensive that there is ordinarily no need to make your own. But in emergencies, or when commercial ones won't do a particular job, you can improvise sinkers from a variety of materials.

A tiny, irregularly shaped rock will make a temporary sinker if the leader can be tied to it without slipping. Attach it to the line about 18 inches above the bait or lure, or on a dropper, so it doesn't frighten the fish.

During my boyhood fishing days, I caught many trout by double half-hitching a simple shingle-nail onto a speckled ten-cent fishing line. A paper clip, part of the emergency fishing-kit, can be bent into a tiny roll and suspended from a dropper leader. A .22 or larger bullet, cut deeply with a knife and then squeezed around the leader, makes an adequate sinker. Similarly, BB shot from an air rifle, or pellets from an air gun, make good sinkers. Even a short length of wire will do in a pinch. Often, lacking a cutting tool as well as a sinker, I have cut a piece of wire simply by pounding it between two rocks.

Special sinker for fishing deep in rocky rivers.

Sometimes commercial sinkers are inadequate in certain situations. As an example, steelhead in Idaho's Salmon River must be fished deep, and the bottom is practically all rocks. This means that a lot of terminal tackle is lost. An angler I know partially solved the problem by developing a sinker with a special shape. It is made from flat sheet lead, approximately ⅟₁₆ inch thick, ⅜ inch wide, and 2 inches long. The ends were tapered by cutting ½ inch off one corner. A tiny hole was bored in one end and a snap swivel attached to allow the sinker to drift along the bottom without twisting.

The sinker is attached to the end of the monofilament line, with the lure attached to a dropper 18 inches up. The sinker is allowed to bump along the river's bottom, with the baited hook above the rocks where there is less danger of snagging. The thin sinker wiggles through most of the crevices without snagging.

Similar long, but round, sinkers can easily be made by cutting off lengths of lead wire—the kind bulletmakers use for the cores of small-diameter bullets —flattening one end and punching a hole in it, and either attaching a snap swivel or threading the sinker on the dropper.

If you really like to tinker, molds are available with which you can cast your own sinkers. Or you can make molds in any shape from hardwood and pour in molten lead.

Replacing Guides

Guides on fishing rods occasionally come off and have to be replaced. If this occurs during a fishing trip, a temporary replacement job can be done with a yard or so of silk thread.

To fix a guide that has become loosened, cut off all the thread windings on both sides rather than try to wrap over them. Then lay the guide in position and hold it in place with the left hand.

Wind the thread around the guide and rod so the end is beneath the turns, as shown in the drawing.

After sufficient turns have been made to bind the thread so it won't unwrap, revolve the rod with the left hand, holding the thread taut with the right. Continue winding past the end of the guide's foot and onto the rod.

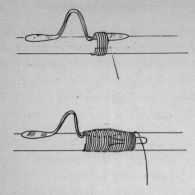

Method of winding thread to replace a rod guide.

To secure the wrap, lay a 3-inch length of thread, doubled, on the wrap before making the last few windings, as in the drawing. The windings should cover this doubled thread almost to the loop. Then pass the end of the winding thread through the loop, and pull the two ends of the doubled thread under the wrap, burying the winding end. Snip off the ends and wrap the other foot of the guide. Coat the fiinished wrap with fly varnish, lacquer, or fingernail polish, if available. Otherwise, the wrap will hold until you get home to apply the varnish.

Replacing a Tip Guide

If the tip guide of a fishing rod comes off, the proper way to replace it is to scrape away all cement on the rod tip, smear the tip with ferrule cement, and replace the guide. Allow to dry before using the rod.

If ferrule cement is not available, you can secure the tip for the duration of a fishing trip by doubling a small length of silk thread over the tip of the rod end and pushing the guide back on. The added thickness of the thread will hold the tip in place.

If the guide is damaged and unusuable, a temporary guide can be made from an ordinary paper clip. Straighten the soft wire of the clip, but leave one of the

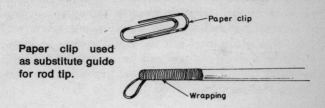

Paper clip used as substitute guide for rod tip.

original bends, forming an eye with two legs. Bend the eye slightly forward. Place the guide in position with the legs under the rod tip, and wrap it in place with silk thread in the same way as in wrapping a guide *(which see)*. Coat the finished wrap with varnish, if available. A bare wrapping will last the duration of a short fishing trip, but a permanent guide should be installed as soon as possible. The soft metal of the paper clip will eventually ruin the finish of a fly line.

Lubricating Ferrules

A jointed fishing rod should be assembled by *pushing* together, not twisting, the male and female ferrules. To unjoint the rod, always pull the ferrules apart in a straight line. Do not twist them. If you can't unjoint a rod alone, get a partner to help you, each grasping the rod on either side of a ferrule. Avoid grasping the rod near a guide; you may strip it off or bend it.

In order to seat firmly, ferrules must fit tightly, but particles of grit or a bit of erosion sometimes cause them to stick. Some form of lubrication is then needed.

Oil is not suitable as it will eventually thicken and worsen the condition.

The best lubricant I've found for ferrules is the natural oil occurring in human hair. To lubricate a ferrule, merely push the male element through your own hair, twisting it and working it around for a few seconds. This will impart just the right amount of lubrication for a day's use and can be repeated each time the rod is used. Of course, as you get older you may have to find another method.

Finding Natural Baits

One of the most available natural baits is the earthworm. It is found in soft soil nationwide. A good place to look for earthworms is along stream banks where the earth is moist but not wet, in farm fields, cultivated gardens, croplands, orchards, and hayfields. Ditchbanks, grassy root areas around irrigated fields, and the ground around small mountain springs also are good places to dig.

Another large white worm, the grubworm, is found in sandy, unplowed areas around cottonwood groves along stream banks. In the spring, sagebrush areas adjacent to stream banks are good places to look for white grubs.

A smaller white worm, the woodworm, is found in old conifer stumps throughout the pine belts of North America. This worm is over an inch long, has a hard, dark head, and lives on wood. You can detect the presence of woodworms by the relatively fresh, round holes appearing in old rotted stumps and logs. Chop into such wood with an ax and you'll find the holes will terminate in sawdust. The worms will be in the sawdust. The wilderness traveler often comes upon rotted logs torn apart by a wandering bear for the ants and woodworms inside. These rotten stumps and logs are a good sign of woodworms.

Ordinary black crickets are good bait. They are often found under rocks and old boards, especially around abandoned buildings. The larger Mormon cricket, which once plagued the agricultural crops of Utah and is now found in many desert areas of the West, is a good bait for large fish. These large, nasty-looking insects can be killed with a long branch stripped of leaves except for a bunch at the end.

Such a stick swatter is the best way of killing grasshoppers, which are one of the best natural baits, especially for trout. Grasshoppers of several varieties are found in sagebrush lands, dry mountain sidehills, and most abundantly in hayfields. The best grasshopper for bait is the small grayish hopper with yellow belly which develops to full maturity from midsummer to late fall. This hopper is just over an inch in length.

If the woods traveler is fortunate enough to locate an old game-kill, or a domestic animal which has died in some outlying range country, and can get to it before predators have cleaned up the remains, he is apt to get a fine bait for whitefish—maggots. These tiny larvae, which develop from the eggs of blowflies and other large flies, are a deadly bait for mountain whitefish. Thread them on a #12 hook.

Several species of flies themselves can be used as bait. The blue horsefly, which is found in most timbered areas in spring and early summer, and whose bite is so painful, is one of these. Threaded on a small hook, and drifted through a pool, it will often take fish.

Hellgrammites are a productive natural bait, especially for mountain whitefish, which will take either the dark or the pale-yellowish species. Both are found on the underside of mossy rocks in stream riffles. The easiest way to catch hellgrammites is to slant a piece of door screen in the water below a shallow riffle, then stir the rocks upstream from it. The insects will dislodge from the rocks and flow down against the screen. A piece of burlap can be used in the same way. Lacking either, simply stir up rocks and pick up the insects as they float downstream.

Small bullheads or sculpins are good bait for large fish. Look for them under large, mossy rocks in shallow riffles. A disturbed bullhead will try to escape under another rock. The best way to catch it is to spear it with an ordinary table fork as it pauses under the edge of the rock. This has now become illegal in some states, so check the regulations. If you are quick, you can catch a bullhead with your hand.

Suckers and minnows are popular baitfish. Try a wormlike strip of meat cut from the shoulder area of a large sucker. Suckers lurk in deep, slow-moving pools and can be caught on worms fished along the bottom. Minnows are the natural food of many species of fish. The easiest way to catch them is with a wire minnow trap baited with breadcrumbs. Lacking a trap, find a shallow eddy containing a school of minnows. Stay out of sight and throw a fist-sized stone into the school. You may stun one or more and be able to scoop them up.

Large trout often go for a mouse bait. Tie the mouse onto a large hook, with the point just below the belly, and allow it to drift into deep pools.

The eggs of large fish make good natural bait, though it is hard to affix them to a hook. It helps to coat the eggs with sugar first, then allow them to dry.

Freshwater clams, which occur in many streams, are good bait for large trout or steelheads. Found in beds, in the deep riffles of large streams, clams can be dug up with a pitchfork. The wilderness traveler will have to use his hands. Open them by cutting the junction of the halves, slice the flesh into strips, and impale them on a large hook.

Removing Embedded Fishhooks

There are relatively few fishhook accidents, since most people are aware of the hazard of barbed hooks. However, occasionally a fishhook will become embedded in someone's flesh.

How to remove a fishhook if point cannot be pushed through skin.

Press down. Pull out.

If the hook is embedded in a finger, ear, or other area with its point nearly protruding from the opposite side, the best way to remove it is to cut the shank, push the point through, and remove the hook. Remove the hook as soon as possible, as there will be a certain amount of numbness and the victim will feel less pain. Numbness may be increased by squeezing the flesh around the hook just prior to removal.

If the hook has sunk into the flesh, and it is not feasible to push the point through, the hook must be pulled out in the opposite direction from which it entered. To pull the hook straight backward would result in the barb sinking deeper into the flesh. Instead, the hook should be held, either with pliers or between thumb and forefinger, and pressed against the skin, as in the drawing. This pressure will open the entrance hole and a quick pull on the hook will usually remove it without undue pain or tearing the flesh.

If this procedure is not possible and a doctor is available, discontinue the fishing trip and seek medical aid, especially if the injury is in the eye area.

Once the hook is removed, the hole should be disinfected. Wash thoroughly with soap and water. Swab well with iodine, mercurochrome, or other disinfectant, if available. The chlorine in such products as Chlorox is a disinfectant. Dilute before applying to the wound.

How Indians Caught Fish

Before the advent of the metal fishhook, the Indians developed several productive ways to catch fish, especially larger species such as migrating salmon, fish in school, or fish in shallow water. They used the bow and arrow to shoot salmon migrating over riffles and in the small creeks during spawning runs. They snagged fish with bone hooks attached to cords, tossing the weighted hook into a pool containing several fish, allowing it to settle to the bottom, then jerking it upward as the fish passed over it.

Spearing fish in shallow water was productive, and several types of crude spears were used. One of the best was made of two pieces of sharpened bone, barbed on the inside, and fastened to the end of a split willow or alder. A thin, triangular piece of hardwood was placed in the split before binding it with cord, to separate the two pieces of bone. The spear was thrust or thrown at a fish in shallow water. If it hit, the

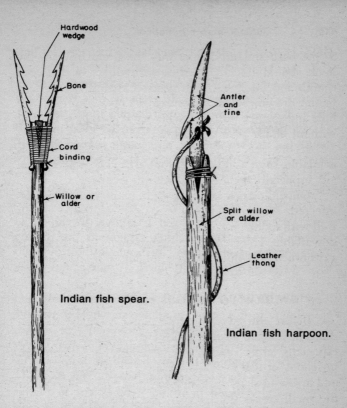

Hardwood
wedge

Bone

Cord
binding

Willow or
alder

Indian fish spear.

Antler
and
tine

Split willow
or alder

Leather
thong

Indian fish harpoon.

barbed edges would prevent the fish from slipping off as it was retrieved.

Small harpoons were used in much the same manner on larger fish such as Chinook salmon, when they could be caught in schools in river pools, or in riffles in spawning creeks. The head of the harpoon was often made of a segment of deer antler, with the tine worked down to form a thin barb. The end of the antler was shaped and inserted into the split or hollowed end of an alder or willow pole, and bound temporarily by a thong. A small hole was then bored through the harpoon head, to which a long leather thong or strong cord was attached. The harpoon was thrust or thrown, and if the head was embedded in the fish, the handle was pulled away, and the fish hauled in by the cord. The harpoon had an advantage over the spear in that it could be thrown farther and both parts retrieved, whereas a heavy fish might carry the spear away.

Indian Fish Wheel

The Indians of Alaska and Canada developed an ingenious device for catching salmon in the muddy and silt-laden rivers of the North where the fish could not be seen or caught with lures. It was called a fish wheel.

The fish wheel was built on a log raft which had an opening in the center to allow the wheel to revolve in the water. The wheel itself contained four spokes radiating from each end of a log axle. The two longer spokes held a pair of baskets woven of willows. The shorter spokes were braced by saplings across the ends. The log axle turned in round notches cut in planks which had been hewn from a log. A log box was built on the raft just behind the wheel.

The raft was placed in the river, against the bank, on a point below a bend. The current turned the wheel on its axle, like a waterwheel, and as the salmon came around the bend and past the point, the baskets scooped them up and dropped them in the log box.

Today, the Indians still use fish wheels of this sort, but the baskets are made of chicken wire instead of willows and the framework is made of lumber. Only the Indians have legal permission to use these fish wheels.

Indian fish wheel.

How Indians Dried Fish

Since the salmon runs were seasonal, the fish caught with the fish wheel had to be preserved to last through the year. Indians of the North dried the salmon. They cut fillets on both sides of the fish, but did not cut through the tail, leaving both fillets hinged together at this point. The fillets could then be hung on a drying rack. After the fillets were stripped from the bones,

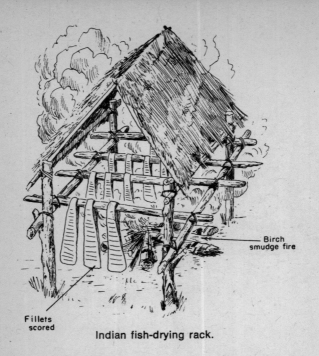

Birch
smudge fire

Fillets
scored

Indian fish-drying rack.

they were scored on the flesh side with lateral cuts of a knife. The fillets were hung on the drying rack with the flesh side out.

Drying racks were built of poles near the fish wheels. The racks were covered with popple branches to form a roof, shading the drying fish from the sun. Sometimes a small birch fire was built under the rack and allowed to smoulder, keeping away the flies, quickening the drying process, and imparting a smoky flavor to the fish. When salt became available, the Indians used it in drying fish. Indians along the Yukon River and other salmon streams of the North still dry their catches in this way.

PART 3

Camping How-To

Making a Safe Camp

The basic consideration in choosing a campsite is the availability of water and wood. A campsite should be *near* a supply of good water, but no so close that it presents a hazard. High shorelines and island-points are good places to make camp. So are knolls in timbered country, and open spots above creeks or springs. The camp should be so located that in case of a sudden storm or flash flood the site will not be inundated. For this reason low river banks, gulley bottoms, dry washes, and similar low areas are not good places to camp.

Similarly, if wood is used for fuel, the camp should be set up close to the supply, but not where timber is a hazard. Tents should not be set under tall, dry trees which may blow over in a high wind—the "widow-makers" of the Northwest. It isn't safe to make camp directly under tall trees which will drip rain or snow on tents and equipment. Moreover, tall trees draw lightning.

The area around any camp should be cleared of brush so sparks from the campfire won't catch. Clearing a campsite of brush also prevents tripping or stumbling, especially at night. Stumps of small saplings should be cut off close to the ground. Paths leading to the water supply, the garbage pit, and the latrine should be cleared of brush and rocks.

The tent should be pitched so that its flap faces the camp area, with its rear toward the timber. Guy ropes should be tied so that campers won't trip over them, and shielded by boxes or other objects. Low, over-hanging limbs are a hazard for woodchoppers and should be cut before anyone swings an ax.

If an open fire is used, the fireplace should be sturdy so that pans of hot water or food will not upset and scald someone. It's also a good idea to keep a large pot filled with water near the fire in case flying sparks hit tarps, drying clothes, etc., and start a blaze.

The chopping block should be set back from the main working area and a firm camp rule established that the ax always be kept sunk in the block. Similarly, saws should be placed out of the way where they will not fall or be tripped over. Unsheathed knives should never be left on the ground.

Orderly storage of food boxes, camp utensils, and personal gear helps to make a safe camp. Items that are out of place, after a camp routine is established, are always a danger. Leveling the ground in the traffic area may prevent such misfortunes as folding chairs tipping over or articles skidding off uneven tables.

Finally, a few simple camp rules should be established by the one in charge: no loaded guns allowed in camp; no fishing rods allowed in the traffic area; no alcoholic beverages allowed before evening. Abiding by a few such sensible rules often saves a camp from tragedy.

Keeping Matches Dry

Here are some ways to keep wooden matches dry in camp:

In a pint fruit jar.

In an empty Alka-Seltzer bottle.

In an empty centerfire cartridge case. Dip the heads in paraffin, and whittle a wooden plug for the case's mouth.

In a hole drilled in your rifle's buttstock. The butt-plate must be removed, the hole drilled, and the plate replaced.

In a plastic wrapping sewed into the pocket of an outdoor garment. Dip the heads in melted paraffin.

In a waterproof matchcase purchased at a camping supplier.

Fire Starters

Fire starters are often necessary to get a poor quality of wood to burn. They may be found in the woods or made at home and taken along.

One of the best natural fire starters is dry pine, spruce, or fir needles. Even during rain or snow, a handful of these can be found on the lower limbs of big trees that will be dry enough to burn well. Such dry needles are reddish in color and easily recognized.

Another good fire starter found in conifer country

is pitch, the resinous substance often found in old stumps. Called "pine-gum" in the West, it is yellowish in color, and in old stumps has the hard appearance of resinwood lamination. If an old stump looks gray, it's apt to be old, soggy, or rotten. If it looks yellow, it's apt to contain pitch.

A few shavings of pitch will start a fire at the touch of a match. Old-timers usually break off a few hunks every time they find a pitch stump, take them to camp, and solve the fire-making problem for the duration of the trip.

The simplest fire starters are a few birthday candles. Half of one of these little candles will be enough to start a fire with even soggy wood. A few of them in a coat pocket weigh practically nothing and won't melt and ruin the coat.

Another good fire starter can be made of newspaper rolled tightly into a half-inch roll, wound tightly with thread, dipped into melted paraffin, and cut into half-inch plugs. The bits of thread which remain act as wicks.

The tiny wax-paper cups used for jelly containers in cafes can be used as forms for making fire starters. Fill the cups loosely with coarse, dry sawdust from a softwood such as pine. Sawdust from a sawmill works

Fire starters can be made by pouring paraffin into blind holes bored in a pine board and filled with sawdust and twine wicks.

fine. Poke a 1½-inch length of old cotton shoelace into each cup to serve as a wick. Pour hot, melted paraffin into the sawdust until the cup is full. The wax causes the sawdust to adhere, and the mixture will burn quickly when the wick is lit.

Small pocket-sized fire starters can be made by boring a series of ⅝-inch holes nearly through a 1-inch, straight-grained pine board. Place a short length of cotton twine into each hole for a wick, and fill the holes loosely with coarse sawdust. If coarse sawdust is not available, the chips made by boring the holes can be used. Allow the twine wick to project through the center of the sawdust. Pour hot, melted paraffin into the sawdust in each hole. After the mixture has cooled and the wax has set, split the board lengthwise with an ax or knife and remove the fire starters from their forms.

Sharpening Axes and Knives

One of the best implements for sharpening an ax was the old-fashioned grindstone, turned by a treadle and cooled by a dripping can of water suspended above it. The old grindstone is largely gone, and today's best tools for sharpening an ax are a shop grinder with an emery wheel and an oilstone. The oilstone is used to put a fine edge on the blade.

When using the grinder, grind slowly so that the temper of the steel is not drawn and the edge is not ground down. Sharpen toward the cutting edge by holding the bit on the grinder so that the wheel turns toward the ax, not away from it. Contact should only be made for a few seconds at a time so as not to generate too much heat.

When finishing the edge with the oilstone, push the stone toward the edge, not away from it, at an angle of about 20 degrees. Some people move the stone in a circular fashion.

Most camp axes are used for felling trees and for splitting wood. The felling bit should be thinner than

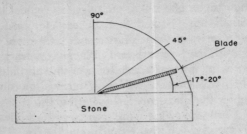

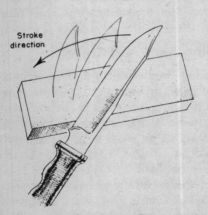

Proper way to sharpen a knife.

the bit used for splitting, but unless a double-bit ax is used, the ax must be a compromise. The bit of most good factory axes will be about right for splitting wood, but will be, or rapidly become, too thick for felling. As an ax wears, and is sharpened only on the edge with a stone, the blade becomes thicker and should be periodically thinned down on a shop grinder.

Knives should be sharpened at home and touched up periodically as they are used at camp. They should never be thinned down on an emery wheel but with a hone or stone.

Most stones for sharpening knives are of carborundum. The larger ones usually have a rough side and a fine side. These are good stones for sharpening knives at home. For field use, a smaller stone such as the official Boy Scout stone is adequate.

The very best knife-sharpening stones are Arkansas stones quarried from natural rock. These come in various degrees of hardness, from "soft" to "hard." A hard stone and a soft one are an unbeatable combination for putting a fine edge on any knife. The stone should be lubricated with a light oil when sharpening. If none is available, water or saliva is an acceptable substitute.

The best stroke for sharpening a knife blade, and the only one to use with a fine knife, is a scything movement toward the user, with the blade held at an angle of 17 to 20 degrees, bringing the entire blade along the stone from hilt to tip. This movement, repeated several times, will bring the edge particles into line on one side of the blade. Then turn the blade over and push it away from you in a similar arc.

An implement long neglected for sharpening fine knives is the "steel" used by butchers. This rod of hard, fluted steel puts a keen edge on a knife in short order. Hold it almost vertically in front of you and stroke the blade down one side and then the other, maintaining the same angle. Steel sizes range from about 18 inches long to a 4-inch pocket model made in Germany. I recently stayed with a professional seal hunter off

Alaska's Afognak Island who could skin a hair seal in three minutes flat. His knives were the best handmade products obtainable, and he would use nothing but a pair of steels for sharpening them.

Chopping Wood Safely

The average camper need not acquire the skill of the professional woodchopper. He will use an ax to fell trees and chop them up for firewood, cut brush around tents, and perhaps hack a trail for a packstring through down timber. There is an art to using an ax which can only be acquired through experience, but anyone can learn to chop safely.

The camper will probably use one of three types of axes: a single bit with a 1½-pound head and 26-inch handle; a double bit with a 2½-pound head and 28-inch handle; a single bit with a 3-pound head and 35-inch handle. The first type is adequate for most wood-chopping around camp. The larger double-bit ax, owing to its longer handle and heavier head, is better if no pounding is to be done. One bit is intended for felling, the other for splitting.

The basic technique in using an ax is to "throw" the head at the target rather than falling on the handle with the body's weight. It is quite like tossing an apple which has been impaled on a stick. Hold the ax over the target and get the "feel" of the situation, as in approaching the ball in golf. Swing the head back, then forward, letting the weight of the ax head do the work.

When felling trees or cutting up long logs, chop at about a 45-degree angle to the grain of the wood. Split wood along the grain.

Before starting to chop, cut away all foliage or overhanging limbs which might interfere with the

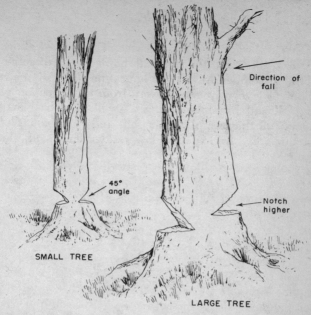

Notch small tree on either side. Cut one notch on large tree lower than other, on side you want tree to fall.

backswing. Don't chop when people are around; the ax head can slip off the helve, or the ax itself slip from the hands. Flying wood is also a hazard.

Cut down standing trees by making opposite notches at the base of the trunk. The bottom of the notch should be cut flat, and at right angles to the tree. The upper surface should slope so that the chips can be "pried" out at the end of each stroke by slightly tipping the bit downward.

Small trees can be cut down by chopping two opposite notches at the base, with each notch reaching approximately halfway through the tree.

With large trees, cut the second notch just above the first notch and the tree will topple in the direction of the first notch. At the first indication that the tree is about to give way, move away from the direction of the fall and from the stump as well. The tree may "jump" off the stump when it falls and strike you. Cut off limbs by striking their lower sides flush with the trunk.

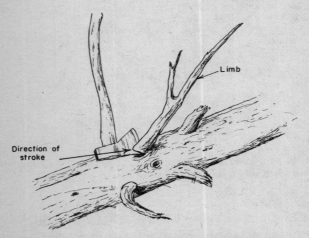

When trimming a large log, cut limbs from this side.

Splitting Wood

The first thing to do before attempting to split wood is to get a large log to use as a chopping block. This block should be large enough to be stable and cut squarely across both ends. When only one end of the block is square, this end should be placed upward and the surface of the ground smoothed so that the block will stand straight. Otherwise splitting wood on it can be dangerous.

All objects around the chopping block should be removed, as they may catch the backswing. If a double-bit ax is used, the bit with the thicker edge is better for splitting. If the bit is too thin, like the edge used for felling, it tends to cut deep rather than to spread the wood.

Chopping
block

Chopping block for splitting wood safely.

There are two basic cuts used in splitting. One of these is "quartering." The log to be split is placed on the chopping block and first cut in half. A small log can often be split with one blow. With larger logs, one blow is often not enough. It is better to strike the first blow at the edge of the block, weakening the wood at this point. Strike the next blow just inside the first blow,

QUARTER CUT

SLAB CUT

Two methods of splitting a log.

further weakening the wood. Successive blows, struck on a line across the center, will eventually split the log. Cut the halves in the same way, as shown in the drawing. Some choppers lay the halves on the block flat side down, and split them this way. This is often necessary when splitting small or knotty logs, or logs with unsquare ends. When splitting a knotty log, try to hit it

Split above knot — weakest part of grain

Splitting a log with a large knot.

above, and in line with, the knot. As this is the weakest part of the grain, the log will split easier.

Experienced choppers often hold the ax in one hand and hold the log half with the other. The trick is to move the hand just before the ax strikes the wood.

A second method of splitting logs is to "slab" the wood, as shown in the drawing. This produces flat boards for making camp furniture or for propping up table legs, etc.

Logs that have been chopped into lengths, rather than sawed, cannot be stood on end to be split. They must be laid on the chopping block, round side up, and quartered.

It is often difficult to split the large, tough-grained logs cut from conifer trees. To make the job easier, find

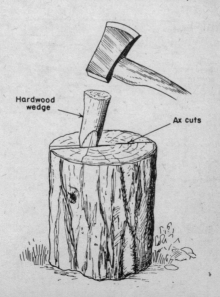

Hardwood wedge

Ax cuts

Use a wedge to split tough-grained conifer logs.

a piece of dry hardwood and make a splitting wedge. In most conifer country, mountain mahogany, maple, or other hardwood is available. Taper a couple of foot-long pieces which are 2 to 4 inches in diameter, making a pair of wedges. Drive the ax into the center of the log end a few times until you can insert one of the wedges in the cut. Pound the wedge into the log with the head of the ax, widening the split, and insert the second wedge. If the wedges are driven into the log at opposite sides, they should split it apart. One wedge, driven into the center of the log, will often do the job.

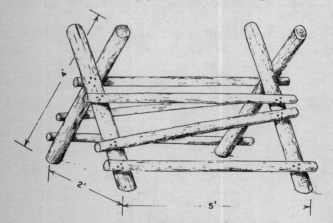

Simple sawhorse for cutting wood at camp.

Sawing Wood

At large camps firewood is often cut up with a portable power saw or with some type of handsaw. The best handsaw for this work is the bowsaw. It is efficient and portable, and is available in lengths from 30 inches up to 5 feet.

The log to be sawed should be rested on a chopping block or log so that the cut is slightly off the block, allowing the weight of the cut-off piece to open the kerf and prevent the saw from binding.

If considerable cutting is to be done, it pays to build a rough sawhorse from small poles found in the area. The drawing shows how a simple sawhorse can be knocked together with a few spikes. The logs are laid in the crosses, and cut beyond the support—again to avoid binding the saw. When the log has been shortened to sawhorse length, saw only until the blade binds

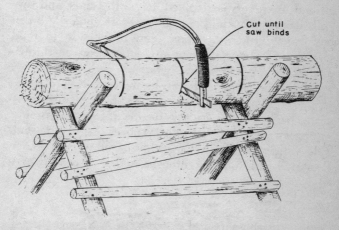

Cut until
saw binds

When log becomes sawhorse length, cut until saw binds, then lay log on the ground and chop from opposite side.

in the wood. Then lay the log on the ground and complete the job by chopping with an ax on the opposite side of each cut. If green wood is cut, binding of the saw can be prevented by smearing the blade with kerosene.

Camp Cupboards

The food supply at camp is often left in packing boxes because there is no lumber available with which to build cupboards and neatly store the supplies. Camp cupboards can be made, however, from the boxes in which the groceries were brought to camp. Also needed are some poles, a few spikes, and baling wire or rope.

A kitchen cupboard should be placed at a suitable working height. Build a stand about 30 inches high of four husky poles sharpened and driven into the ground, two crossbars spiked across the ends, and several slender poles laid on the crossbars. The stand can be placed inside the cook tent, or outside in mild weather. If a storm comes up, a tarp can be thrown over the cupboard.

The cupboard itself can be made of several types of boxes. The cardboard cartons in which grocery stores pack supplies are suitable. So are wooden orange or apple crates, or a few alforjas boxes. Turned on their sides, and placed in a row on the stand, the boxes can be stored with food and utensils so that an orderly cup-

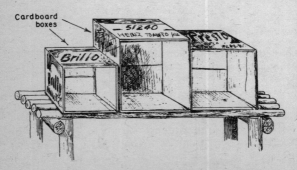

Cardboard boxes serve as camp cupboards.

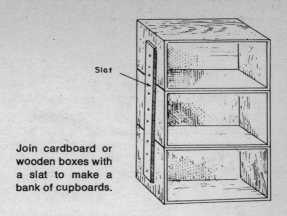

Slat

Join cardboard or wooden boxes with a slat to make a bank of cupboards.

board is avaliable to the camp cook. If enough boxes are brought to camp, a double-decker cupboard can be arranged, with the second layer covering the joints of the first. Place the heavier items in the lower row of boxes and the lighter supplies on top. If the boxes are light or flimsy, they can be reinforced with a small slat as shown in the drawing.

Several types of boxes are available at large military surplus stores which can easily be converted to camp cupboards. One of these is the bomb-kit container; another is the portable officer's field desk. These boxes are of plywood with metal binding and are light and rugged. They make fine containers for hauling food in cars and boats, or on packhorses.

Camp Tables

A rustic table built of native materials is far more stable and roomy than the folding card table often taken along on auto-camping trips. The table can be made in two ways. One is simply to construct a stand similar to the one previously described for supporting a camp

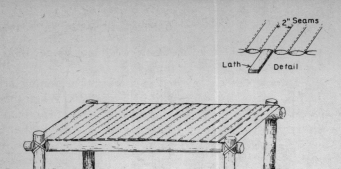

Roll-up camp table of seamed canvas and lath.

cupboard. If it is to be a large table, built with heavy corner posts, it is not necessary to sharpen the posts and drive them into the ground. They can be cut square at the ends and stand upright. In this case, side rails should be nailed or lashed to the posts to give the table stability. The poles used for the top should be slightly flattened on top and bottom to lie flat and provide a smooth surface. They are nailed or lashed to the crossbars.

If the corner posts are driven into the ground, seats can be built integral with the table, but a third pair of posts should be used, one on each side between the corner posts, for added stability. Nail or lash three poles to the ends of the corner posts at a height of 18 inches. These poles should extend 18 inches beyond the corner posts on each side and form the supports for the benches. Several slim poles of suitable length are then nailed to these supports.

A portable top for this camp table can be made from a length of 3-foot canvas of 10-ounce weight and wooden lath. The canvas should be 1 foot longer than the desired length of the table top.

Double the canvas and sew seams, beginning at the fold, across the width at 2-inch intervals. When the seams are made, cut lengths of wooden lath 1 inch shorter than the width of the canvas and insert them into the pockets formed by the seams. Then sew the open end of the canvas, locking the laths in the pockets. Finally, sew a pair of cloth tapes to one end. In storage or transit the canvas can be rolled into a tight bundle and tied with the tape. At camp it is unrolled on the framework of the table and forms a stable top.

Camp Stools

Unless you are auto-camping, chairs and stools are hard to transport. However, several types of stools can be made at camp which, although short on upholstery, are rugged and provide seats for tired campers.

The traditional camp stool has always been a short log, broad enough to make a seat, and cut square at

Simple camp stool — a slab nailed to a log.

each .end. But in areas where large-diameter logs are not available, a stool can be fashioned from a slim log and a slab of wood cut as shown in the section on splitting wood. Smooth both surfaces of the slab and nail it to the log.

Camp stool made from a half log fitted with legs.

At a semipermanent camp where tools can be packed along, fancier stools can be made of split logs. The logs should be at least 12 inches in diameter and about 18 inches long. After splitting a log, bore a pair of holes at each end, angling inward. Cut four small saplings for legs, about 15 inches long, preferably of green hardwood, and pare down the ends to fit in the holes. If the holes have been bored at an angle, the legs will spread and you'll have a sturdy stool.

Homemade Baker Tent

To make a baker tent the following materials are needed:

1 piece of canvas 3 by 36 feet.

1 piece of canvas 6 by 6 feet.

From the 36-foot length cut three pieces, each 11 feet long. Sew them together to form a rectangle 9-by-11 feet in size. Hem the edges of the sheet along its 9-foot sides, and fit grommets at the corners and sides if desired. This is the roof of the tent.

Cut the 6-foot square of canvas diagonally, forming two equal triangles. Sew the long side, or hypotenuse, of each triangle to the long sides of the roof, with the tip of the triangle flush with the edge of the roof. These form the sides of the tent.

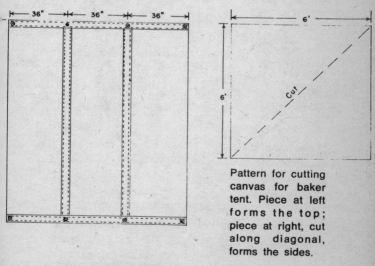

Pattern for cutting canvas for baker tent. Piece at left forms the top; piece at right, cut along diagonal, forms the sides.

On the underside of the roof, a few inches above the point where the sides end, sew four large loops of hemmed canvas. These should be large enough to admit a 4-inch ridgepole, as shown in the drawing.

Sew loops for tent pegs at the four corners and midway between. (If the canvas has been fitted with grommets this is unnecessary.) Sew two loops on the lower side of the roof, 2 feet from the bottom edge and 2½ feet from each side. Small guy ropes tied to these loops and pegged to the ground will prevent the roof from sagging.

The finished tent may be waterproofed with a

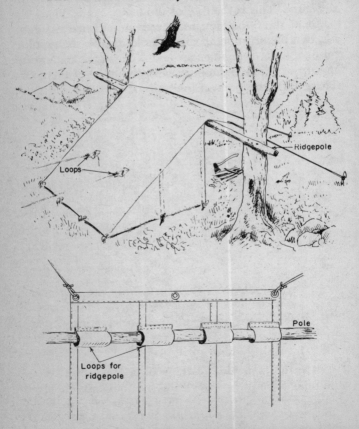

Baker tent erected between two trees. Detail shows loops sewn on underside of roof to admit the ridgepole.

commercial solution applied according to the directions, or with paraffin. To waterproof the tent with paraffin, shave 2 pounds of paraffin into a container and heat to melting. Next, heat a tubful of water to the boiling point. Remove the tub of water from the stove and place it outside or at a safe distance. Into a smaller container pour 2 gallons of white gasoline. Place the container of gasoline into the tub of hot water. As gasoline has a lower boiling point than water, the gasoline will boil. Pour the melted paraffin into the container of gasoline. Fold the tent loosely and immerse it in the gasoline-paraffin solution. Allow it to soak for a while and then hang it on a clothesline until the scent has gone.

Lantern Case

The glass-globed gasoline lantern provides excellent illumination in camp, but it's a fragile piece of equipment to transport safely. The simple lantern case shown here will protect a lantern from the jouncing it usually gets in transit. It was built for a Coleman single-mantle lantern. Adjust the dimensions to fit your own.

Cut the sides of the case from ¼-inch plywood. These are screwed to the corner posts, which are cut 1½ inches shorter than the sides. Allow the sides to overlap the posts ¾ inch at each end. Cut the bottom of ¾-inch plywood or pine, of a size to inset the sides, and screw it at the corners to the ends of the posts. The lid, also of ¾-inch stock, is cut to fit flush with the case edges. Cut another piece the same size as the bottom, and screw it to the underside of the lid so that it insets the case. Attach the lid to the case with strap hinges, and add a hasp and handle.

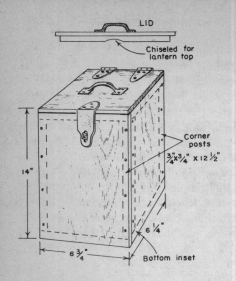

LID

Chiseled for lantern top

Corner posts
¾" x ¾" x 12 ½"

14"

6 ¼"

6 ¾"

Bottom inset

Case for holding camp lantern tight during travel.

If the box is the correct size, the top of the lantern should just prevent the lid from closing. Chisel a small depression in the underside of the lid to fit the lantern's top, thus holding it snugly in the case. Finish the case with a couple of coats of varnish stain, perhaps dark oak.

With the lantern well fitted, such a case can be transported in any position and absorb the usual bumps encountered on an outdoor trip.

Alforjas Boxes

Alforjas boxes were originally designed to fit inside the canvas panniers used with sawbuck packsaddles. They are also useful for packing personal belongings on camping trips in cars, boats, and airplanes. An added advantage is that these light boxes can be used with packsaddles without panniers by simply lashing them to the saddle with a sling hitch. To be most useful, alforjas boxes should be built to fit into panniers, whose dimensions are somewhat standardized. The box shown in the drawing meets these specifications, and it is easy to make.

Half-inch lumber, or ⅜-inch plywood, is used for the sides and bottom, and 1-by-10-inch lumber for the ends. The ends can be cut in a mild V-shape to conform to the side of a horse, as in the drawing, or left straight. Use flatheaded wood screws or cement-coated 6d box nails for joining the sides and bottom to the ends. Attach a 1-by-2-inch cleat to each end of the box with four screws. This cleat slants to allow the lash ropes to run from the front ring of the saddle under one cleat, across the front of the box, under the other cleat, and back to the rear saddle ring. When the lash rope is drawn tight with the completed sling hitch and tied, the box will ride securely on either a Decker or a sawbuck packsaddle.

The corners of the box can be reinforced with brass corners, or with rawhide which is soaked and shaped to fit, and tacked solidly in place.

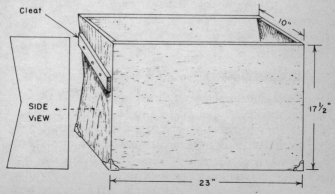

Alforjas box with V-shaped ends to fit horse's side.

Packhorse or Car Kitchen

It is often desirable to have cooking equipment and basic food items packed and ready to go at a moment's notice for an overnight camping trip. Building a pair of camp kitchens is a good solution.

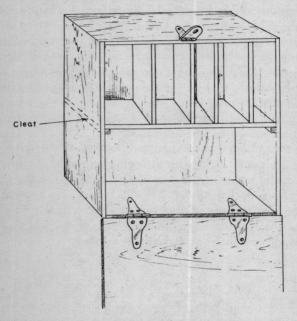

Cleat

Camp kitchen should be compartmented for neat storage.

If you live in a region where packtrips are common, the kitchens should be built to fit panniers. A suitable size is 24 inches long, 18 inches high, and 10 inches thick, or wide. One of the best materials for the end pieces is 1-by-10-inch planed lumber. A good material for the bottom and both back and front is ⅜-inch plywood. If very heavy material is to be carried, ½-inch plywood is better for the bottom.

The kitchen differs from an alforjas box in that the top is closed, and the front is hinged at the bottom and anchored to the top with either a hasp latch or a window latch. The advantage of the hasp is that it may be padlocked. Two-inch strap hinges are used to attach the front panel to the bottom.

The inside of each kitchen is fitted, according to the user's needs, with plywood shelves and upright cubbyholes. Usually the lower part of the box has no partitions, leaving space for storing large items. The upper half is partitioned into small sections to hold plates (vertically), cups (nestled), knives and forks, condiments, etc.

At camp, the kitchens are simply lifted off the pack animal or out of the car or boat, and the front opened. Everything inside is ready for immediate use. Often when table room is at a premium, the kitchen can be set on a block and used as a table. A pair of restraining chains, one at either side, can be attached to the front to hold it in a horizontal position.

Emergency Jack

At camp it is often necessary to move large logs or rocks that are in the way. On the road, your car may get stuck in the mud so badly that the car jack can't dislodge it. In both situations, it's possible to make a jack with only a length of ½-inch rope and a couple of poles.

One pole is a 3-foot length of stout log, cut square at one end. The other is a pole 12 to 15 feet long and 3 to 5 inches in diameter. Cut a shallow notch in this pole about 3 or 4 inches from the larger end. Stand the small log upright on its square end and lash the pole to it. Hold the pole at right angles to the upright and use a diagonal lashing, finished off with several turns of frapping. The lashing should be somewhat loose so that the pole will not bind.

The result is a long lever attached to an upright. The height at which the lever is placed can be regulated by shifting the lashing up or down the upright. In use, stand the upright log on a flat rock, a patch of hard ground, or a wood slab. Point the long end of the lever skyward, and hook the short end under the vehicle or object to be moved. Lift the object as high as possible, and block it up with logs. Move the lashing upward on the upright, and take another "bite." Repeat until the object has been lifted as high as is necessary.

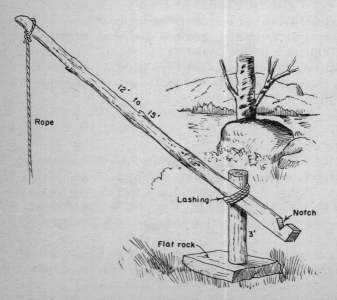

Rope

12' to 15'

Lashing

Notch

3'

Flat rock

Emergency jack for moving big boulders or stuck vehicle.

You can get an even longer "bite" if a piece of rope is attached to the end of the long pole. The pole can then be angled higher, giving greater leverage.

Saw-Blade Covers

Exposed saw blades can cause nasty wounds, and ruin tents, bedrolls, and other camp gear. Saw blades should have some kind of protective cover during transit and at camp when not in use.

One of the simplest saw-blade covers is a length of burlap or a gunnysack. If the burlap is wrapped around the blade and tied with cord, only a very violent blow will cause the teeth to penetrate. Start the wrapping at one end of the blade, with a corner of the sack. A good cord for tying the material in place is butcher's cord, the kind used to tie salami ends.

A better-looking and long-lasting cover can be made from cardboard carton material. Cut a 3-inch strip the same length as the blade, and fold it lengthwise. Insert the blade and tie the cardboard in place with several pieces of cord.

For short saws, a length of rubber or plastic garden hose makes a fine blade cover. Cut the hose the same length as the blade, then split it along its full length. The split hose, slipped over the saw blade, is fastened with cord every few inches.

The blades of long crosscut saws can be transported safely enclosed between two lengths of ¼-inch plywood, slightly larger than the blade size and at each corner.

Extra blades for bowsaws can be safely carried in tight rolls packed in flat cardboard boxes or wrapped with several turns of burlap and tied solidly. The rolls should be tied securely with wire before they are pack-

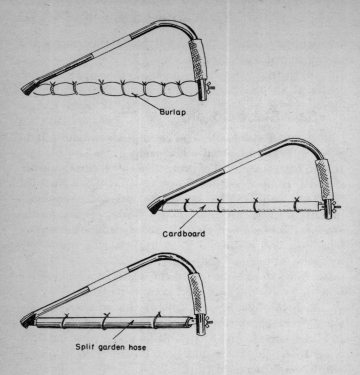

Burlap

Cardboard

Split garden hose

Three types of saw-blade covers.

aged. A rolled bowsaw blade that springs loose is a
hazard to everyone nearby.

Making Ax Sheaths

Ax blades should be kept covered in transit or at
camp. Not many ax makers supply sheaths, but you
can make your own.

A good sheath for a double-bit ax can be made
from two small sheets of heavy-gauge steerhide, sev-

eral copper rivets, a length of light leather strap, and a small buckle.

First, draw a pattern on heavy paper of the two sides of the sheath. These sides should be exactly the same shape and size. It is necessary to make two to achieve a precise fit around the curves of the blade. An allowance for the rivets of ¾-inch should be left at both edges and along the underside.

Trace the pattern of the two halves onto the leather and cut them out with a sharp knife. Then rivet the two pieces of leather together around the edges of the bit and along the underside, leaving a space for the handle. Space the rivets 1 inch apart. The top of

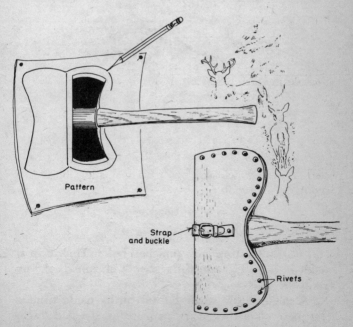

Pattern

Strap and buckle

Rivets

Sheath for double-bit ax.

the sheath is left open. Copper rivets-and-burrs are the most lasting fasteners for joining the leather sides. The two-element rivets available at 5-and-10 stores are nearly as suitable.

After riveting the two sides, rivet a small buckle to one side of the sheath. On the opposite side, rivet a

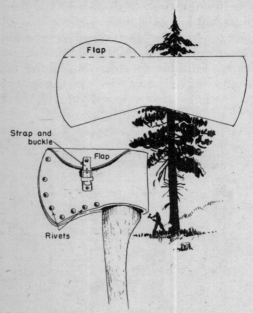

Sheath for single-bit ax.

short length of strap with punched holes. This strap is buckled across the top of the sheath and holds the ax solidly in place.

A sheath for a single-bit ax can be made from a long piece of leather, or two smaller pieces if a single piece is not available.

If one piece of leather is used, draw a pattern on heavy paper as shown in the drawing. Allow ¾ inch at the edge for riveting. The flap is optional. If two pieces of leather are used, cut two patterns, leaving enough leather at the back to be able to rivet the sheath over the butt of the blade.

If the sheath is made of two pieces, rivet on a strap and buckle similar to the one on the sheath for a double-bit ax. If a flap has been cut on one side, fold it over the face of the ax and rivet a short strap to it. Then rivet a buckle to the side.

Knife Sheaths

The short sheaths that are sold with many knives are not entirely safe for strenuous activities such as horseback riding and climbing. The knife often slips from the sheath and is lost or stabs the wearer during a bad fall. It is easy and inexpensive to make a rugged sheath that will fit most types of knives.

For an average-size knife, a foldover sheath of heavy, stiff steerhide is durable and safe. It should be long enough to cover the entire blade and most of the handle. Only enough of the handle should protrude so that the fingers can catch the butt and pull the knife from the sheath.

Draw a paper pattern to fit the knife, leaving sufficient room at both edges for riveting or lacing, and transfer it to the leather. Cut the leather and soak it in warm water until it's soft. With a blunt tool, such as the end of a folded pocketknife, form-fit the softened leather to the knife. This is done by inserting the knife into the folded leather, and carefully molding the leather to its shape. The important areas to work down are the hilt and along the grip itself. If the leather is somewhat soft, the approximate shape of the knife can be imparted to the sheath.

Next, carefully remove the knife without disturbing the flexible, shaped sheath and allow the leather to dry. When dry, the sheath may be riveted or laced along the edge to a point just above the hilt. Care should be taken that there is enough room in the sheath to admit the hilt but that it will fit tightly.

Small, hammer-on rivets may be used, but they will enlarge the size of the finished sheath. It is better to lace the open side of the sheath with a length of ¼-inch buckskin, or similar soft leather such as the lace known as tooling calf.

Before lacing, holes must be punched in the edges of the open face of the sheath. These should be approx-

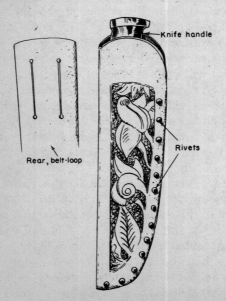

Sheath for hunting knife.

imately ³⁄₃₂-inch holes, spaced ¼ inch apart, and stag-
gered along opposite sides.

An overhand lacing is simplest for the beginner.
Experienced leather workers may use one of several
types of edge stitching. To begin the overhand stitch,
lay a couple of inches of the lace between the halves of
the sheath at the bottom end. The first stitches will be
around and over this length of lace, binding it down
firmly and out of sight. Continue lacing the edges to
the finishing point at the approximate middle of the
grip. It is easiest to complete the lacing without regard
for tying in the end. Then with an awl or nail loosen
the last half-dozen stitches, poke the end of the lace
under these stitches and between the edges of the
sheath. Starting with the last tight stitch, tighten the

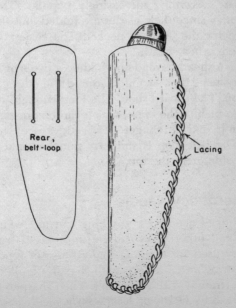

Rear,
belt-loop

Lacing

Sheath for folding knife.

loosened laces again. At the last stitch, a loop will occur. Pull the loop under the final stitches, as with whipping a rope end, and cut it flush. This conceals both ends of the lace and prevents it from unlacing.

A belt loop may be riveted on the rear side of the sheath. However, to prevent the knife from slipping out of the sheath it is better to cut the belt loop in the sheath itself. To cut the belt loop, make two rows of tiny holes 1½ inches apart, with ¾ inch between the rows. Then slit the leather between the holes. The loop should be cut so its lower end is just above the hilt. When the belt is inserted, the inside of the leather loop will bear against the grip of the knife and hold it tightly.

Folding sheath knives, shaped like large pocketknives, are becoming increasingly popular. They are safe to carry since their blades are folded, but they are too large for the average pocket. The easiest way to carry them is in a sheath.

Such a sheath is made by folding a piece of leather to fit the knife, then lacing it around the edges, nearly to the top. The sheath should be long enough to cover all but an inch of the knife, which can be grasped with the thumb and forefinger. The edges are laced as above. The belt loop is similarly punched and cut in the rear side, near the top.

Emergency Needle

A rugged needle for patching canvas, sewing soft leather, and other tasks can be improvised from the metal key used for opening many types of food cans. Simply straighten the key with a pair of pliers, and pound it straight with a hammer. Then sharpen the tip with a small file. Lacking a file, use a small sharpening

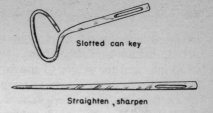

Emergency needle
made from slotted
can key.

Slotted can key

Straighten , sharpen

stone. Tarps, tents, bedroll covers and other camp gear
can be repaired with such a needle, using cord, fishing
line, or leather laces.

Tent Bags

When camping in a tent on an extended trip, it is
difficult to keep personal articles in order. A tent bag
for keeping shaving kit, toothbrush, extra socks, and
other items handy can be made of a piece of canvas. A
good size for such a bag is 20 by 24 inches. To make a

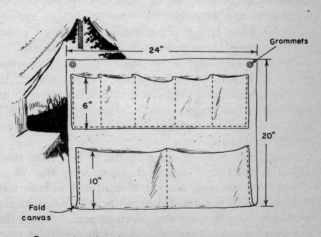

Canvas tent bag keeps personal articles in order.

bag of that size you'll need a piece of canvas 24 by 30 inches, and another strip about 6 by 24 inches.

First hem the edges of the larger piece of canvas. Then fold the 30-inch side to form a 10-inch pocket at the bottom. Stitch the edges and sew a seam up the middle, dividing the pocket into two compartments. Sew the smaller strip of canvas 3 inches from the top, stitching it along the bottom and at both ends. Then sew vertical seams at intervals, separating the pocket into five or six compartments. Finally, set grommets into the top edge 2 inches from each corner. The bag can be hung from nails driven into one of the poles that support the sides of a wall tent.

Bough Bed

The air mattress and the folding camp cot have made outdoor sleeping a comfortable experience. There are times, however, when an air mattress springs a leak, or when backpacking in the wilderness it's necessary to improvise a mattress from conifer boughs.

Cut several armfuls of green boughs from small spruce or other conifer trees. The boughs should be about 18 inches long and thick with foliage. Begin by making a pillow approximately 3 feet wide and from 8 to 10 inches thick. Starting in the middle, lay individual boughs so that the butts point outwards.

Then lay more boughs on the pillow with their butt ends touching the ground. These are placed at an angle of 45 degrees, leaning toward the pillow. Lay each succeeding row of boughs at the same angle, pressed tightly against the previous row, so that the tips stand a foot off the ground and form a thick mat. Continue laying rows of boughs until the bed area is completely covered. For the bed to have a comfortable

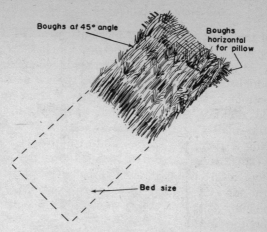

Boughs at 45° angle

Boughs horizontal for pillow

Bed size

How to lay boughs for a camp bed.

spring to it, sufficient boughs should be used. If there are not sufficient boughs in an area, it is best to make the shoulder area thick and skimp on the foot. Or place a small log on each side of the bed to prevent the boughs from spreading under your weight.

Leaf Bed

During the fall season, when leaves are shed, a wilderness camper can gather dry leaves and use them for insulation and softness under his outdoor bed.

Leaves, unlike thatched boughs, will not remain in place during the night but will slip from under the sleeper. To prevent this, make a bed frame of four logs, as shown in the drawing. The side logs can be placed 30 inches apart. The cross logs are cut to bed width, then spiked inside the side logs at proper length. It helps to make notches on the outside of each side log, then

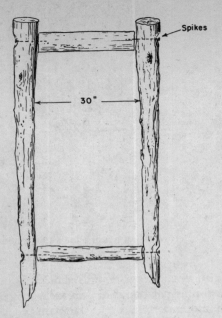

Wooden frame for a leaf bed.

drive the spikes through these into the ends of the cross logs.

If the logs for the frame are about 6 inches thick, or even larger, they will prevent the leaves from scattering. Level the ground inside the frame, pile the leaves inside and smooth them down. The blankets or sleeping bag are placed on top.

Grass-and-Pole Bed

If the ground where you want to make your bed is wet, you can make a mattress of grass and poles. First make a bed frame as described for a leaf bed. On top of the frame, place small, dry poles fairly close togeth-

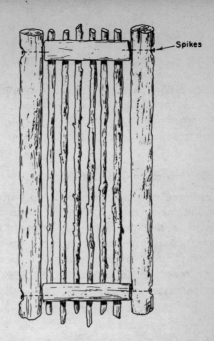

Spikes

Wooden frame for a grass-pole bed.

er, and lash or nail them to the end logs. Small jack-pine, lodgepole pine, or spruce poles are suitable. Then invert the entire framework so that the poles attached to the frame become the bed's bottom. Place the framework so that the head is slightly uphill. Sometimes it will be necessary to smooth the ground and pile dirt higher at one end.

Finally, spread grass or leaves inside the framework, and lay the bag or blankets on top. The poles will protect the sleeper from moisture in the ground, and keep the leaves from scattering. This type of framework and mattress also can be used on snow or sheer rocks.

Bales of straw or alfalfa hay used similarly will make good outdoor mattresses. Horseback hunters often divide a bale of hay for mattresses, and then feed it to the stock on the last day of the hunt. A camper who is near farmland can arrange to get ample mattress material from a stubblefield or haystack.

Dead-Man Tent Stakes

Tents are normally staked down with commercial tent stakes, or wooden stakes cut from saplings and sharpened on the spot. However, when a tent must be set up on sandy ground, or snow, or on a gravel bar, stakes won't hold. In such places the best method of staking a tent is to use a "dead man" at each corner.

A dead-man tent stake is merely a stick of wood, a

Log anchors tent rope securely in sand.

long rock, or even a long chunk of ice tied to the tent's guy rope and buried in the ground. For an average-sized tent, a dead man 18 to 24 inches long will be ample, even in sand.

Dig a hole where each dead man is to be placed. The depth of the hole depends on the softness of the footing. In pure drift sand, a hole 2 feet deep will be ample. Tie a length of wire, rope, or strong cord to the center of the object to be used as an anchor. This should be long enough to extend above the ground after the dead man is buried. Bury the dead man in the hole and tamp the earth over it. Then tie the rope to the loops of the tent.

I have watched Eskimos stake fox traps in snow with this method. They set the trap, then ran the wire from the trap's stake chain into a hole in the snow.

With the small oil stove they melted snow in a pot and poured it slowly over the length of wire in the hole. It only took moments in that 30-below-zero temperature for the water to freeze solidly into a bar of ice along the hole's bottom. They carefully tramped snow on top, immobilizing the trap. When timber is not available, a winter camper can use the same procedure to pitch his tent on snow.

Trenching a Tent

It's a good idea to trench your tent, even though it doesn't look as if it will rain. Especially in mountainous country, sudden showers often occur during the night and an inundated tent takes a bit of the fun out of camping.

If the ground on which you have chosen to pitch your tent slopes slightly, pitch the tent with its rear uphill. You should sleep with your head toward the rear of the tent.

With a shovel, ax blade, or sharpened board, dig a small trench around the tent. The trench should be about six inches from the back and side walls and extend beyond the front. Keeping the trench close to the tent will prevent anyone stumbling over it. Pile the dirt from the trench along its outer edge, forming a little dike. This small dike of dirt, spread evenly around the tent's back and sides, will divert water flowing downhill. Water coming off the canvas will run into the trench and around the outside of the tent. Bevel the ground between the tent walls and the trench to keep water from running under the tent.

How to Dispose of Garbage

Bury all tin cans, food remains, and other garbage which will eventually disintegrate and become part of the soil. When burying garbage, dig the pit far enough from camp to avoid flies or odor, and deep enough so that when it's covered with dirt, bears and other animals will not be able to unearth the garbage and scatter the remains.

Garbage that will burn should be sorted out and piled in an open area where there will be no danger of setting a forest fire. If part of the refuse is wet and won't burn, it is permissible to pour a little gasoline from a lantern onto the pile and start the fire by tossing a match onto it from a distance. When the fire is blazing well, stir it with a stick until everything is burned. Take care that the fire does not become too large and cause an accident.

Garbage that won't burn or disintegrate in the ground, such as glass bottles, should be taken home or disposed of in barrels provided in many camping areas. In some of the remaining wilderness areas, campers are now required to do this. In the Bob Marshall Wilderness Area in Montana, for example, campers are required to pack out all glass bottles and tin cans—anything that won't burn.

Camp Toilet-Paper Holder

A 2-pound coffee can, nailed through the bottom into a tree next to the latrine, will keep toilet paper dry at camp. The can should slant slightly downward to prevent rain or snow from dripping off the trees and into the can. Owing to the length of the can, it is hard

Coffee can nailed to tree keeps toilet paper dry.

to drive the nail with a hammer. The best way is first to punch a hole in the bottom from the outside. Then, while holding the can in position, insert the nail into the hole and drive it into the tree by holding the end of a short limb against the head and hitting the protruding end with a rock.

Simple Camp Utensils

Making extra dishes around a camp is easy. A plate can be made by slabbing off an inch-thick board from a length of pine log and shaving down

Method of shaving a slab to make a dish.

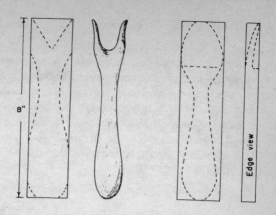

Fork and spoon whittled from slabs of wood.

the top surface with an ax. Hold the head of the ax in one hand and push it like a block plane over the face of the board, shaving it until it becomes smooth. It is not necessary to remove the bark on the edges.

To make a knife, use a 6-inch length of any small, dry hardwood limb, shave a 3-inch "blade" with a pocketknife, and round off and bevel the edge. The knife will cut butter and spread it, cut boiled meat and similar food, and even steak if it is tender.

Similarly, a usable fork can be made of an inch-thick slat of straight-grained pine, spruce, or Port Orford cedar. Cut the slat to about 8-inch length, and flatten 2 inches at one end to nearly ⅛ inch thickness. Next cut a V in the end 1½ inches deep and hollow out the tines. Smooth the edges and surfaces of the tines and shape the handle. It is best to make the tines first; if they break it is easier to begin again before working on the handle.

If there is a 20-inch length of galvanized wire in camp, as well as a small file, a fine fork can be made for heavy work such as turning meat or pick roasting corn from the coals. Bend the wire at the middle to form a U. Then twist the two ends together into the shape of a fork. Sharpen the tines with a file or stone so they will spear large pieces of food. Be sure to clean the fork after meals, otherwise the metal may contaminate food.

Simple cooking fork made from a length of galvanized wire.

Wooden spoons for cooking and eating can be carved from a slab of wood 1 inch wide and ½-inch thick. This slab may be cut from any straight-grained wood, but a pine split is best. About 1½ inches from the end, carve a spoon blade by first making a notch on the top side, then tapering the bottom side from a point 1½ inches back to the tip. Shape the flat blade to form an oval and carve the handle to the rough form of a spoon. If you have the time and inclination, you can use soft wood and hollow out the blade.

Camp cups are easy to make from new tin cans. Cut the can through the center, leaving an inch uncut at the seam. Then make two vertical cuts so that a strip of metal about 1 inch wide is left, extending from the can's center to the top. Hammer a fold in the raw edge of the cup and pound it smooth. Do the same with the edge of the strip. Then bend the strip into the shape of a handle.

Edges folded→
and hammered

To make a camp cup, cut tin can along dotted line, fold and hammer edges.

Small frying pans can be made in the same way from gallon-sized fruit cans. Coffee- and teapots can be made from any tin can of suitable size by adding a wire bail. Punch two holes on opposite sides at the top of the can and twist the ends of the wire through these holes. The length of the wire should be about twice the can's diameter to form a loose loop. A good wire for this purpose, and one of the handiest items around any camp, is ⅟₁₆-inch copper wire. It is strong but easily bent with the fingers.

Camp Tongs

A pair of tongs is handy around an outdoor camp for moving coals, logs, hot pans, and other tasks. A pair can be made in a couple of minutes

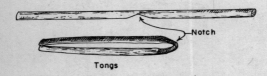

Wood tongs serve many useful purposes around camp.

from a green stick. The stick should be cut twice as long as the desired length of the finished tongs. Cut a notch at the center about two-thirds through the stick. The sides of the notch should form a wide angle so the stick will fold. Flatten the inner side of each end to aid in gripping objects.

Doodle Hook

Another useful wooden tool around an open cooking fire is a doodle hook. Made from a green, forked stick, it is a handy tool for lifting the heavy lid of a hot Dutch oven, a pot of boiling coffee, or a pail of hot water from the fire. If the end is sharpened, it can be stuck in the ground near the fire and always be ready for use.

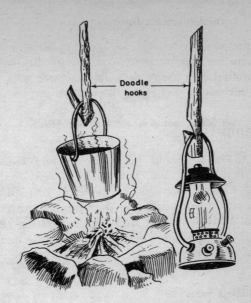

Two types of doodle hooks.

In areas where green wood is unavailable, another form of doodle hook can be made from a length of dry wood about 18 inches long. About 2 inches from one end cut a deep notch. The upper edge of this notch should be long and sloping, the lower edge short and steep. Hook the notched stick under the handle of a pot or lantern and use it as a lifter.

Walloper

If you dislike cleaning greasy pots and pans with your hands, make a walloper. All you need is a dishrag or pot scourer, a 10-inch stick, and a nail.

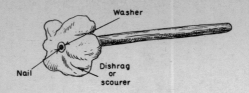

Walloper cleans dishes in a jiffy.

The stick should be approximately ¾-inch in diameter, peeled and smoothed. Simply nail the dishrag to the larger end of the stick, first folding it so the nail head won't pull through. To prevent the mesh of a metal scourer from slipping off the head of the nail, cut a washer of leather, or whittle one from a small piece of wood.

Camp Toaster

One of the best camp toasters is simply a length of forked alder or willow. If the fork is cut to a

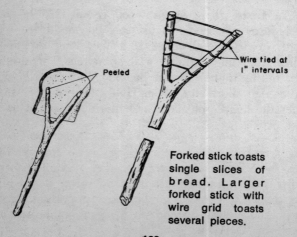

Peeled

Wire tied at 1" intervals

Forked stick toasts single slices of bread. Larger forked stick with wire grid toasts several pieces.

3-inch spread, the tines will hold a slice of bread firmly. A 2-foot handle prevents burning the hands. Simply impale a slice of bread on the tines and toast it over coals.

Another toaster, for holding several slices of bread, can be made from a larger forked alder or willow. The fork should extend a foot or more from the main branch at about a 45-degree angle. Tie pieces of wire across the fork, at 1-inch intervals, forming a grid. This grid will hold several slices of bread for toasting over coals.

Grub List

Because of individual requirements and preferences, there are as many grub lists as there are campers. No single list could possibly fit everyone. One husky camper may want meat three times a day; another may want fruit. The way to make up a grub list that will satisfy everyone and provide balanced meals is to use the principle of multiples.

First figure the number of meals anticipated during the trip. Say there will be three fellows going, and the camping trip is for four days. This means there will be twelve breakfasts, lunches, and suppers. Incidentals will be left until later.

The next step is to begin with a basic menu for one of the day's meals—say, breakfast. A good outdoor breakfast consists of orange juice, bacon and eggs, hotcakes, coffee, and perhaps a small dish of fruit. This basic breakfast is then broken down into one-person servings. This is most important, since the total amounts depend on the reasonable accuracy of this estimate.

A 6-ounce serving of juice is reasonable. Three strips of sliced bacon, or about 3 ounces, is average. Two eggs per person. One good recipe for hotcakes calls for 1 egg with enough milk to make 1 cup mixture, into which is stirred 1 cup of prepared pancake mix. This will make 6 large pancakes, approximately 5 inches in diameter. So for the individual's hotcakes, there will be ½ egg, ½ cup of milk (or ¼ cup of canned milk diluted with ¼ cup water), and ½ cup of hotcake flour. Butter and syrup, jelly, or jam are normally used on hotcakes. One ounce of butter is ample, and 3 ounces of syrup will do. One ounce of granulated coffee will make what a normal person wants for breakfast, as will ½ ounce of sugar, and 1 ounce of canned milk. Let's assume that the fat from frying the bacon will cook the hotcakes, and that 1 pound of salt and a can of pepper will last the entire trip. Also, figure 6 ounces of canned fruit to a serving.

Multiply all individual servings by 12 and the result would be the following breakfast list:

Orange juice—72 ounces, or about 4½ pints

Eggs—2½ dozen

Hotcake flour (prepared)—6 cups or about 3 pounds

Butter—12 ounces, or 1 pound with a bit extra for frying

Syrup—36 ounces, or a bit over two pints

Coffee—12 ounces, or for practical purposes, 1 pound

Sugar—6 ounces, or around ½ pound

Canned milk—30 ounces, or 2 large cans and 1 small can

Canned fruit—72 ounces, or about 4½ pints

This is a reasonable estimate of what three

people would eat for breakfast for four days. Next comes the remodeling of the list to suit individual tastes and requirements.

For instance, the menu might be altered to have ham instead of bacon for two breakfasts, so an estimated amount of ham is included and a proportionate amount of bacon is left out. If one person eats only one egg for breakfast, the egg total is revised accordingly. Perhaps only two people eat canned fruit after their hotcakes, so only two-thirds of the fruit total is included. One person may like tea for breakfast instead of coffee. If he uses 2 tea bags each time, then he'll need 8 tea bags, and the coffee total may be cut down one-third. If jam or marmalade is used on hotcakes half or the time, then the syrup total may be cut, and the jam estimate added. In many instances, in good fishing or hunting country, there is a possibility that fresh fish or liver and onions may be used for breakfast, instead of bacon, eggs, and hotcakes. This may be anticipated, but should never be depended on. Finally, in estimating a grub list, include those items that make camp eating so much fun—such as a cookie or two after the morning coffee.

The other meals are planned in the same way. When the total amounts are figured for twelve breakfasts, lunches, and dinners, *all* should be increased as much as 25 percent to have ample food in case of emergency.

Using a Space Blanket

One of the finest items recently developed for campers is the space blanket, a sheet of fiberglass enclosed in two layers of material and used principally as an insulator. Many blankets are silver on one side and red or blaze-orange on the other. The blanket is lightweight and can be folded into a pocket-sized package.

A space blanket is waterproof to the extent that prolonged dampness will not penetrate it. It can be used as a ground cloth for sleeping, or as a cover for duffel or a packboard load during a sudden rain, or as a seat while trail watching on damp ground.

But it is as a wrap that the space blanket is most useful. Draped around the shoulders Indian fashion, so that it creates a kind of "tent," the blanket will keep you warm in the chilliest weather. The Indians understood the principle of insulation and used a blanket in this way when they wanted to keep warm. Their body heat warmed the space inside the draped blanket and insulated them from the cold. Any blanket will keep a camper warm, but the advantage of the space blanket is that it's light and made of the best insulating materials.

The red or blaze-orange side of the blanket is designed to serve as a safety wrap on a deer stand. The average olive-green camp blanket camouflages a hunter too well, and he's apt to be mistaken for a deer. Wearing a blaze-orange space blanket is a good precaution.

The blanket is also useful as a signal flag in an emergency. Tied high in a tree or on a long pole, and waving in the breeze, it can be seen from an airplane and from over a half-mile away on the ground.

Transplanting Trees and Shrubs

Have you ever come upon a fine specimen of small spruce, pine or fir in the mountains and visualized it growing on your home lawn? Here's how to transplant it:

Choose a small tree or bush for transplanting, one that has a symmetrical shape. It makes no sense to transplant a ragged tree. It will not improve through the years.

The tree must be removed without disturbing the roots or exposing the taproots to air for too long. The best way to accomplish this is to transplant the tree without removing the dirt from the roots. Spring is the best time to do this, before summer growth begins and the sap begins to flow freely.

Dig a small, circular trench around the tree,

Three steps in transplanting small tree.

gradually going deeper until you've dug under the roots. With small trees no higher than 2 feet a block of earth 15 inches in diameter will be adequate.

It will be difficult to remove the tree without the soil breaking away from the root system unless some kind of container is used. I have found that the best container is a half-bushel peach basket. When the tree is sufficiently loosened in the ground, lift it out with the shovel and, steadying it with one hand, place it in the basket. Shovel fine dirt into any spaces between the root dirt and the basket and tamp it down with the handle of the shovel. This is important, as it seals off air from the exposed root ends. Then slowly pour a bucket of water around the base of the tree. This helps to settle the earth and further seals the roots from air.

When the tree has been firmly implanted in the basket, carefully move it to the site where it will be transplanted. It is wise to decide in advance where you want to transplant the tree, to avoid having to rectify a mistake by digging up the tree a second time.

Having chosen the exact spot for the tree, dig a hole the size of the basket. Then lower the basket into the hole by the handles. Tamp dirt around the outside of the basket and slowly pour another bucket of water over the buried roots. After the water has settled, sift a little dirt over the top, sealing off the air.

With proper care, a transplanted tree will "take" in the earth. As the roots begin to grow again, the wooden basket will decay and the new roots will grow through it. In a few years the basket will be completely decayed and the tree firmly rooted in the ground.

How to Bank a Campfire

When sleeping near the heat of an open fire in cold weather, you must bank the fire to last through the night. This means it must be arranged so as to protect the coals from an undue amount of oxygen.

Build the fire an hour or so before retiring and allow it to burn down to a bed of coals. Shovel a ring of dirt around the fire about the height of the coals. Then sprinkle the dead ashes which are left at the edges of the fire over the top of the coals, covering them completely with a thin layer. Banked in this manner, a fire will burn and emit warmth for several hours. The dirt and ashes will admit just enough oxygen to keep the fire burning without completely smothering it. To replenish the fire, scrape the top away and place a few bits of dry wood onto the remaining hot coals. Fan the coals with a hat, or blow on them. They should blaze up and ignite the wood.

How Indians Carried Fire

The Indians had no matches to start a fire with a flick of the wrist, so they often carried their fire with them from one campsite to the next. They used the hollow horn of a buffalo or wild sheep as a container. After cleaning the inside of the horn, they filled it with fine ashes from the fire, added coals on top of the ashes, and more ashes around and on top of the coals. The ashes insulated the horn so it wouldn't get hot, and kept air from the coals so they wouldn't burn up. Keeping the horn in an upright position, the Indians were able to carry their fire great distances. When they reached their new campsite, they prepared a bed of dry tinder, poured the hot coals on top, and fanned the smouldering wood into a blaze.

Plastic Water Carrier

In semiarid regions the water supply may be some distance from a suitable campsite, and water must be carried a considerable distance. If you are backpacking and have only small utensils, this can become a real problem.

A square sheet of plastic neoprene, often used to cover packboard loads, makes an excellent water carrier. Tie the opposite corners of the sheet with a square knot. Then push the sheet into the water until

How to use a plastic sheet to carry water.

it fills. Grasp the two knots and lift. The sheet forms
into a bag and may be carried half full of water.

A 4-foot-square sheet of heavy neoprene will
make a bag capable of carrying at least 2 gallons. I
have carried water in such a bag for over a half-mile
out of a rocky canyon without much loss. The bag
may be hung from a suitable tree limb in the shade
and used as a permanent water container.

If the water situation ever becomes critical, and
it is necessary to catch rainwater, a large sheet of
neoprene is useful. Such a sheet is often used as a
tent floor or lean-to shelter. Lay the sheet on the
ground in an area where its center will be a bit lower
than its edges. If necessary, the edges can be
propped up with rocks or dirt. Rain will gravitate
toward the sheet's center, where it can be dipped up.

Using Clorox Bottles

A handy item to have around camp is an empty
plastic Clorox bottle in half-gallon size. It can be
used as a water jug, and if you are in doubt about
the purity of the water supply, it will disinfect the
water at the same time. Chlorine, which this product
contains, is often used in tablet form to disinfect cu-
linary water, and the commercial product will work just
as well as the tablets.

The ratio is eight drops of Clorox per gallon of
clear water, and twelve drops to the gallon if the water
is turbid. If a half-gallon bottle of Clorox is emp-
tied at home and held upside down for about ten
seconds, there will be just about the required four
drops remaining on the bottle's inside. If the empty
bottle is taken to camp and filled with water, the
water will be disinfected.

Cut Clorox bottle along dotted line to make boat bailer.

Because of its plastic construction and inset handle, the bottle stores well among other types of dishes and cooking utensils without danger of breakage. Such a bottle is especially useful for carrying fresh water in a boat.

This bottle also makes one of the best boat bailers imaginable. To make the bailer, leave the cap on the bottle and cut the lower end in the form of a sugar scoop, as shown in the drawing. Grasp the bailer by the handle and scoop the water out of the boat. The plastic material will bend a trifle and can be forced into corners where a metal can won't fit.

Camp Coat Hangers

The sportsman who leaves the city wearing a business suit, and travels by plane, boat, or automobile to a fishing or hunting camp, rarely finds a place to hang his dress wear when he arrives. His suit usually ends up in a pile under his cot.

A simple coat hanger can easily be made from a curved, dry limb around 18 inches long. Remove the

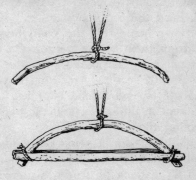

Simple coathanger (top) holds pants with addition of two sticks tied at each end.

bark, and scrape off the fuzz which is common to dry wood, otherwise it will shed particles on the garment. Cut a small notch in the center of the hanger's underside and suspend it from a loop of cord. With the coat on the hanger, the ends of the cord can be tied around the tent's ridgepole or looped over a nail.

A pants bar can be added by tying a straight branch to the ends of the hanger. Two bars will keep the press in the pants better than one.

Hauling Ice Water in a Car

When traveling in desert regions it is necessary to take along a sufficient supply of water, and if you want to preserve fish or game birds on the return trip you'll need ice as well. With the new plastic collapsible containers, it's possible to have both. These containers come in 1-gallon and 5-gallon sizes. For one-day trips a couple of gallon-size containers will suffice, but for trips of several days in very hot weather you'll need the 5-gallon size.

Before leaving home, fill the containers nearly to the top, and put them in the freezer. On the trip, when water is needed it is poured from the containers of ice, which will be slowly melting. If you have an insulated cooler to keep food supplies, the containers can be kept in the cooler and the packages of food piled around them.

The ice will keep for a remarkably long time. On a one-week fishing trip in Baja California, six of us took along 85 gallons of frozen water in these collapsible containers. We had enough drinking water for the week, and had enough ice left to preserve several coolers full of tuotuava and corvina steaks and butter clams.

Indian Tipis and Wigwams

The Indians built many different types of dwellings—pit houses, log houses, pueblos, tipis, and square wigwams, to name a few. Of them all, the tipi seems to have taken the strongest hold on our imagination, for when we think of Indians, we generally think of them living in tipis.

The tipi was used by many different tribes, especially by the nomadic hunters of the Great Plains and central Canada. As every schoolboy knows, it was a conical-shaped framework of poles covered with animal skins or bark. The Plains Indians used buffalo hides to cover their tipis; the Canadian Indians the skins of caribou. When a tribe moved from one hunting ground to another, they often dragged the poles of their tipis behind their horses and used them again.

The tipi was constructed by tying three slender poles near the ends, standing them upright to form a

Indian tipi.

tripod, and then leaning other poles against the top with their ends fitted in the crotch. The base of each pole was planted firmly in the ground. Space for an entrance was left at the front of the structure. If

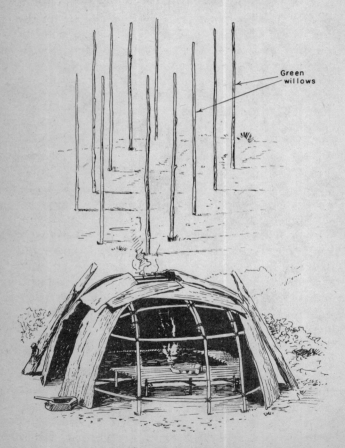

Square wigwam.

birch bark was to be used as a covering, large sheets were cut by girdling a tree in two places and cutting away the bark in one piece. These sheets were flattened and sewed around the framework.

The Indians understood the principle of the draft and chimney, and left an opening in the top of the tipi. The low entranceway provided draft for the fire, which was built in a stone pit in the center of the dirt floor, and the smoke escaped through the opening in the top. The Indians eventually discovered that smoke flaps at the top greatly improved the draft; these were added by extending the covering material to form V-shaped flaps on each side of the opening. If more draft was needed, the bottom edges of tipi covering were raised.

In regions where there were no trees to make tipis, but where willows were available, certain tribes made square wigwams. The framework of these wigwams consisted of numerous long willows, sharpened at the ends and implanted in the ground on the four sides of the wigwam's perimeter. If the willows were long enough, they were bent over to form a canopy and their tips buried in the ground. Wigwams were made of shorter willows by bending them in from each side and fastening them where they overlapped. This framework was covered with bark, skins, or blankets. The fireplace was located in the center of the wigwam, and the smoke escaped through an opening in the top. A low entranceway provided the draft.

A wilderness traveler can easily make such a square wigwam in willow country and cover it with neoprene plastic sheets, tarps, or canvas. A simplified "covered-wagon" wigwam can be built more easily by using willows on only two sides and fastening them at the top.

Indian Steam Bath

Before the first white men came to North America, the Indians had discovered the many mineral springs throughout the land and bathed in them regularly to cure their ailments. The same springs were used for generations, and today many spas stand at the sites of these early Indian health resorts.

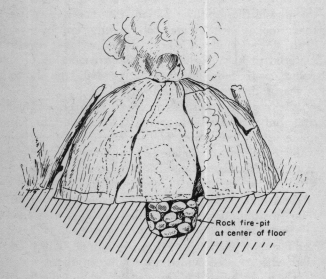

Rock fire-pit at center of floor

Indian steam bath.

In Idaho, Lava Hot Springs and the Mud Baths along the Salmon River attract many visitors. Years ago I visited a hot spring in British Columbia, along the Liard River, which Canadian Indians had once used. I hiked to the spring along an old, worn Indian trail.

When they were unable to visit a mineral spring, the Indians often built their own steam baths for curing aches and pains. These baths were small, square wigwams with a rock firepit in the center. The bather sat on a block of wood, with his head above the framework if he wished. The fire in the pit was kept burning until the rocks were hot. The bather then got inside, poured water over the rocks, producing steam, and closed the entranceway.

Campers with time on their hands can easily make an Indian steam bath in willow country, using canvas tarps or neoprene sheets for covering the wigwam.

How Indians Made Rabbit-Skin Blankets

A singular talent of the North American Indian was his ability to use almost everything in his environment to supply his simple needs. In the Far North, for example, the Indians used the skins of the abundant snowshoe rabbits to make warm blankets. In winter the pelage of this rabbit (actually a hare) turns white—a camouflage coat in the snowy landscape. At this time the skin is at its prime and does not shed its hair.

The rabbit skins to be used for a blanket were stretched and dried, and cut into long strips. The strips were cut in two ways. With a flat skin—that is, one that was split along the belly line—the rough edges were cut off and the circular skin cut in a spiral, starting from the edge and working toward the center, until the entire skin was cut into a single strip. If the skin was removed in one piece, or "cased," so that it formed a tube, the strip also was

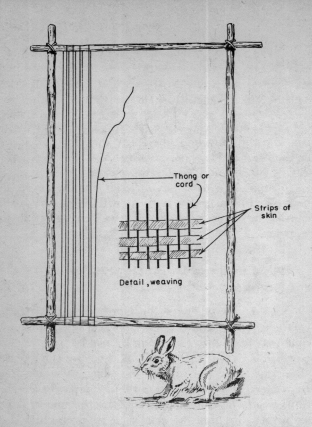

Wood frame laced with thong or cord formed warp for weaving blanket of strips of rabbit skins.

cut in a spiral, starting at the tail and working toward the head. The latter method saved a little of the skin, and the strip tended to curl less.

The frame on which the blanket was woven was simply a rectangle of poles lashed at the corners. This frame was wound with a long thong cut from the hide of a deer, moose, or caribou, forming a warp on which to weave the blanket. The rabbit skins were then woven through the thongs of the warp, the end of one skin being sewed to another as the work progressed. When the entire warp was filled, the thongs were cut from the frames and tied together to prevent the blanket from unraveling. These rabbit-skin blankets were so warm that the Indians continued making them even after woolen blankets were available from The Hudson's Bay Company.

Driving a Nail with a Handkerchief

This may sound like a magic trick, but it's actually a simple method of driving a nail into a tree if you lack a hammer or a rock. It's always handy to have a few nails in trees around camp for hanging gear.

Fold a handkerchief until it is about 2 inches square. Place it in the palm of your hand, holding it

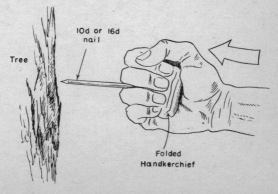

Handkerchief folded in palm cushions hand.

so it won't unfold. Grip the nail between the second and third fingers, with the head held tightly against the handkerchief. Now stand about a foot in front of the tree, draw back your arm, and punch the nail into the the tree much as a boxer throws a body punch. A strong blow will drive a 10d or 16d nail at least an inch into the wood. Don't try it with shorter nails; you're liable to bruise your knuckles against the bark.

PART 4

Cooking How-To

Balanced Meals

There are outdoor chefs who can prepare meals that rival the creations of a hotel chef working in a modern kitchen with the latest appliances. I have been nourished in the outdoors by such delicacies as barbecued trout, T-bone steaks, baked potatoes with sour cream, blueberry pancakes made from wild berries picked on the spot, braised ptarmigan, baked salmon, and cakes, pies, and pastries of every description.

The average outdoorsman need not be able to cook such elaborate dishes, but he should know what constitutes a balanced meal and should master the basic techniques of outdoor cooking so he can prepare edible and enjoyable meals over a campfire or portable stove.

A balanced outdoor meal should contain proteins, carbohydrates, fats, and vitamins. The outdoorsman with limited cooking experience will find it easier to remember these components in terms of actual foods—meat, potatoes or macaroni, vegetables, bread and butter, fruit. Obviously the same menu can't be repeated at every meal because people demand variety. Eggs will furnish the protein at breakfast, if meat isn't served. Hotcakes will replace bread and butter. Juices, instead of fruit, will provide vitamins. Rice may be substituted for potatores or macaroni. A good stew may contain everything except dessert.

With the many prepared foods available to campers today, anyone who likes the outdoors can learn to cook well enough to get by for the duration of a trip. All he needs to know is how to make acceptable coffee or tea, cook such staples as bacon and eggs, read printed recipes, and use a can opener. It helps if he understands what each of the basic cooking processes does to food, and can cook simple foods with a minimum of utensils. After that, to become a fine outdoor cook he only has to buy a good outdoor cookbook and follow directions. The real secret is practice.

Cooking Fires

The advent of such fuels as propane, butane, and gasoline for portable stoves, and the current popularity of camping vehicles, has greatly reduced the need for the wood cooking fire. Nevertheless, there are many times when the outdoorsman must use wood for cooking, particularly in wilderness areas. Outdoorsmen have cooked their food over hardwood, softwood, willows, brush, sagebrush, and even buffalo chips.

Most outdoor cooking fires are used before they are ready. The cook builds a fire, and when it is burning well he begins to cook. Generally speaking, this is wrong. The fire should be allowed to burn for a considerable time until a bed of hot coals is formed. Coals provide a more uniform heat and will not blacken utensils as badly as will flame.

When wood fuel is used in a camp stove, it isn't necessary to let the fire burn down to coals. The metal of the stove, and the confinement it gives the fuel, induce a regular heat while the fire is burning. But in an outside fire, blazing wood, especially in a strong breeze, produces an erratic heat which alternately cooks and cools. A bed of hot coals produces an even heat which the cook can regulate simply by shifting the cooking utensils.

To stabilize the cooking heat further, it is best to use heavy utensils. A heavy griddle, Dutch oven, or skillet won't heat up as quickly as a thin steel skillet but it will hold heat long after it has been removed from the fire. This helps to maintain an even cooking heat with no danger of flash burning the food.

A further way of controlling the heat from an outside cooking fire is to use some kind of grid over the fire. This may be an old refrigerator or oven shelf supported by rocks placed on either side of the fire, a homemade steel grid with legs, a small sheet of metal, or merely two rows of rocks flanking the fire, set close enough together to support a pot. One of the best grids available in conifer country is a pair of green logs of similar diameter placed on opposite sides of the fire. When the coals are ready, they are raked with a stick into the opening between the logs. The pots and pans are placed on top of the logs. Logs 3 feet long and from 6 to 8 inches in diameter are fine for this purpose.

Frying Foods

To fry foods means to boil them in oil. The amount, or depth, of the oil is important. Foods may be fried in shallow oil, as when cooking bacon or steaks. Or foods may be deep-fried—plunged into deep boiling oil and completely covered. Such foods as shrimp, doughnuts, and French-fried potatoes are often deep-fried.

Frying is a poor form of cooking compared with other methods. Frying coats pieces of food with a layer of fat which is digested late in the digestive process, largely through the action of bile. Despite this fact, frying is much used in outdoor cooking because it is easy, quick, and tasty for foods such as fish and steak. The newer shortenings and frying oils are better than the old standby lard, since food does not absorb them as much and they drain better after cooking. Also, people engaged in vigorous outdoor activity have hearty appetites and good digestive systems. Fried foods rarely cause them discomfort.

However, the amateur outdoor cook should still try to keep fried foods to a minimum, alternating with other forms of cooking. For example, if fried ham has been served for breakfast, roast or boiled meat for supper would be better for health.

Boiling and Stewing

Another form of cooking is boiling. Such camp foods as vegetables and less desirable or tougher cuts of meat often are boiled in water to which salt has been added. Butter, flavoring, and condiments may be added after the food is cooked. A tough cock sage grouse, or the leg cuts of an elk or moose, can't be tenderized by frying. But boiling them for several hours will render them edible. Often a piece of tough meat is boiled for a time, then fried to make it more palatable.

Care should be used used in boiling tough meat of any kind. If the cooking water is brought to and kept at a rolling boil, it often tends to toughen already tough meat. Instead of boiling, it is far better just to simmer the meat and water.

This leads us to another form of cooking—stewing. Stewing is a good cooking method for the outdoorsman, especially if he isn't in a hurry. A stew can be set on the coals, a little dry wood added now and again, and gradually cooked over a period of several hours. Stewing preserves the juices of meat and vegetables which are lost in other forms of cooking.

There are two things to remember when making any kind of meat-vegetable stew:

First, the ingredients should be placed in the pot to cook in the order of their toughness, or the length of time it takes to cook them. For example, tough meat should be started first, and raw carrots added before such items as diced potatoes or cooked string beans. Such flavoring as catsup, or a can of tomato sauce, would be added last.

Second, the stew should not be allowed to reach a full boil but be kept at a bubbling simmer. Simmering, in addition to tenderizing the meat, retains the flavor of the stew. A final virtue of stewing is that a good stew gets better as it goes along. What is left over from a big supper is just as good when heated up and served at breakfast.

Elevation affects cooking time for both boiling and stewing, since water boils when the vapor pressure equals the atmospheric pressure. Thus at sea level the boiling point is higher than it is at high altitudes, as anyone who has boiled eggs above timberline in the Rockies has discovered.

Baking

Baking is a cooking process which employs hot, dry air as the heating medium rather than hot fat or water. The outdoorsman normally uses one of a few basic utensils for baking: the oven of a sheet-metal camp stove, a reflector oven, or a Dutch oven. A substitute for a Dutch oven can be made by inverting one heavy cast-iron or cast-aluminum skillet over another of the same size. If a good fit is obtained, the air inside the oven will be heated evenly.

At some large camps that are used annually, and at some western ranches, outdoor ovens are built of brick, cinder blocks, or native stone. These have grates inside and are equipped with steel doors—somewhat on the order of the outdoor adobe ovens that Indians in the Southwest have used for decades. These large ovens are ideal for baking large quantities of bread and cakes, and an understanding of their construction and use will help the camper who must use a smaller oven for baking.

Besides bread and pastries, apples, potatoes, fish, ham, and squash can be baked. These foods are often smeared with a thin layer of melted butter or shortening before placing them in the oven. This thin layer of fat or butter not only keeps the food from scorching on the side that touches metal, but it also imparts a better flavor to the crust.

For the average camper, the primary thing to remember in baking is to produce an even heat around the food and to maintain the heat long enough to bake the food without scorching it. This takes experience.

The stove oven and the Dutch oven maintain an even heat throughout. A reflector oven, which is open-faced, depends on an even flow of heat from the hot coals in front of it. To produce the maximum degree of reflected heat the top and bottom faces of the oven must be set at about a 45-degree angle to the coals.

Roasting

Roasting is a form of cooking in which food is subjected to heat from an open fire. As with baking, hot air is the heating element, and is radiated over the surface of the food. The food often rests on a metal roaster or pan and is covered so that moisture and juices will not be lost. The juices are condensed by contact with the upper part of the container and drip back on the food, a kind of self-basting which prevents scorching or burning.

The American Indians used to roast food in many simple ways. Birds, fish, or pieces of meat were placed on the end of a forked stick and held before an open fire. Again, entire birds were often wrapped in heavy mud and placed in hot coals to cook. Then the caked mud was removed, exposing the cooked, moist meat. Ears of corn were similiarly roasted in mud.

The Indians of the Southwest used the roasting process as a military expedient. In the rimrock country of Arizona, I have repeatedly come upon huge pits full of blackened embers. When an Indian tribe was being pursued by white soldiers, they often sent their squaws ahead to dig these pits, line them with coals, and roast the trimmed, gourdlike bodies of agave and century plants. When the retreating braves came upon the pits, cooked food was awaiting them. The soldiers, having to extend themselves with packed gear, often could not catch up with the braves, who traveled light and found their food along the way.

Today, Boy Scouts often roast food in such simple ways when learning survival techniques. But practically speaking, the camp cook generally will roast meat on top of the camp stove, inside a camp oven, or in a Dutch oven on the hot coals of a campfire.

Broiling and Barbecuing

Other methods of cooking outdoors are broiling and barbecuing. Broiling means to cook over an intense heat, usually a flame, and normally is used for meats. In the home electric or gas oven, the heat usually comes from above; at camp the heat usually comes from below.

Broiling is a good way to cook meat at camp. Portable charcoal broilers can often be taken along. If meat is seared on both sides, then cooked a bit more slowly until done, the charcoal imparts a delicious flavor.

Barbecuing, of course, is a specialty at western ranches where outdoor pits are often built. An entire animal, such as a sheep or a small pig, or perhaps a large piece of beef, may be barbecued in one of these pits. This entails building a fire hours in advance to create enormous quantities of hot coals. The food is wrapped in wet burlap, canvas, or large green leaves and placed in the pit on the hot coals. The entire pit is then lightly covered so that moisture will not escape.

A covered barbecue "pit" may be built above ground from two halves of a steel drum or steel culvert. The lower half, set on legs and equipped with a grid, contains the charcoal. The upper half is hinged to the lower half so that it can be closed on the coals and food. I recently had the pleasure of eating some prime beef which had been barbecued in such a "pit" at the famed Y-O Ranch in Texas. A huge piece of beef was barbecued for five hours, then served with the trimmings and a special barbecue sauce.

Tempering a Griddle, Skillet, or Dutch Oven

Three of the most useful camp cooking utensils are a large griddle, a skillet, and a Dutch oven, all of cast iron. Most camp foods can be cooked in one of these three utensils. Generally the griddle is used for cooking bacon, eggs, and hotcakes, the skillet for frying a variety of foods, and the Dutch oven for baking or roasting.

Before using any of the three utensils for cooking, old-timers would "burn them in," or "temper" them. To temper a new griddle, either of cast iron or cast aluminum, place it on a stove and heat it for about an hour. Then cover the entire cooking surface with some form of fat. The best thing to use is the rind from which bacon slices have been cut. If a large piece of rind is not available, a small amount of cooking oil may be used.

With the griddle hot, and the surface covered lightly with oil, use a spatula to smooth down the cooking surface. This surface may appear to be entirely smooth, but it will have tiny particles of metal which will cause food to stick unless they are worked down. Invert the spatula, as shown in the drawing, and push the blade repeatedly across the entire cooking surface of the griddle. Apply a fair amount of pressure, and be sure to scrape the corners as well as the center.

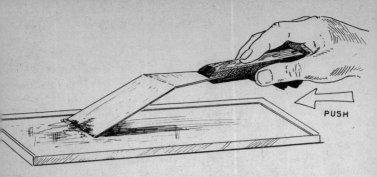

PUSH

Tempering a griddle with a spatula.

During the scraping, the oil or grease will become slightly blackened from minute particles of metal and dust from the factory surfacing. Wipe the griddle surface clean two or three times during the tempering, and apply more oil or grease.

After an hour of such scraping a new griddle will be ready for cooking hotcakes. When finished, wipe the griddle with a paper towel or dry cloth, but *do not* wash it with water. After future uses do not wash the griddle but coat it lightly with bacon rind or cooking oil and dry it with a cloth or paper towel. Food particles that stick to the surface are burned off by heating the griddle and then drying it while a light film of cooking oil remains on the surface. The light film of fat or oil will work into the pores of the metal and food will not stick to it. It will also prevent rusting. And the hot oil cleans just as well as soap and water.

A Dutch oven may be tempered in much the same way. It is heated, lightly oiled, and heated again until the cooking oil or fat smokes. Then it is wiped with a dry paper towel or dish cloth. The walloper described previously is a good tool for doing this without burning the hands. The underside of the lid is tempered in this way, as well as the bottom part of the oven. An occasional light coating of oil or bacon fat applied to the entire surface will keep it from rusting. This should be done especially before traveling or when storing the oven for long periods of time.

The best Dutch oven for baking bread is not the modern one with its rounded, convex lid, but one of the older models with a rimmed, concave lid and three legs. The legs keep the oven level on a bed of coals, and also raise it slightly above the coals if desired. The rimmed lid is nearly airtight and designed to hold hot coals in its concavity. These produce an even heat inside the oven, even when it is removed from the coals.

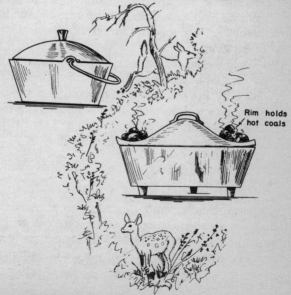

Rim holds hot coals

Two types of Dutch ovens. Older model, right, has concave lid for holding hot coals.

Many campers take along a few charcoal pellets and use them for this purpose.

Baking Bread and Biscuits

Loaf bread is baked in a Dutch oven in the same way it is baked in a home oven. The loaves are formed, allowed to rise, then coated with melted butter and placed in the hot oven. It takes practice to get the heat just right, but if the oven is set on a firm bed of hot coals, just at the side of the fire, and its lid filled with hot coals, bread will bake in approximately one hour without burning.

Fresh biscuits are always welcome in a camp. If a stove is not available, biscuits can be easily made in a Dutch oven. They are mixed, formed, and baked just as in the home oven.

Biscuit mixes, with all ingredients already in the flour, are available at any grocery store. One of the best, especially for the lazy camp cook, is a product called Krustease which mixes with water and forms a stiff batter. The beauty of this product is that it will also make hotcakes, dumplings, and waffles.

Doughnuts

A special treat around a camp on a rainy day is a batch of doughnuts. Here is a fine recipe which calls for fresh (not sour) milk, so diluted canned milk can be used. The recipe will make forty-eight doughnuts.

1 cup sugar
3 teaspoons baking powder
2 tablespoonfuls melted shortening
2 eggs, slightly beaten

1 cup fresh milk, or ½ cup canned milk mixed
    with ½ cup water
½ teaspoonful vanilla flavoring
1 teaspoonful salt
½ teaspoonful cinnamon
½ teaspoonful nutmeg
⅛ teaspoonful ginger
4¾ cups flour
½ teaspoonful lemon flavoring

Mix and blend the eggs and sugar. Sift the flour
and mix with the salt, spices, and baking powder. Then
add milk, shortening, and flavoring to the flour mixture
and mix into a dough. Chill the dough. Roll the chilled
dough on a floured board into a sheet about ¼ inch
thick.

Cut the sheet of dough into doughnut shapes with
an empty tin-can top—about 2¾ inches in diameter—which has been floured. Break the center of each
doughnut with the fingers into a rough hole. Immerse
the doughnuts in approximately 3 to 4 pounds of boiling lard or cooking oil, turning when done on the bottom side, and cook until done. Allow the doughnuts to
drain on a paper towel and sprinkle with sugar. Save
the hot fat for other uses.

Southern Fried Pies

A fine camp recipe for a cold, snowy day is a batch
of southern fried pies. A regular pie-crust dough may
be used, or the same one used for doughnuts. The
filling is made from packaged raisins.

Plump two cups of raisins by putting them in 1½
cups of cold water, add 1 tablespoonful of butter, and
boil for one to two minutes. Next, stir 1 cup of sugar

with 3 tablespoonfuls of flour and a few grains of salt. Add enough water to the sugar-flour mix so that it can be stirred. Stir this mixture into the raisins and allow to boil for two to three minutes, stirring constantly. Remove from the heat and allow to cool slightly.

Cut the dough into circles about 5 inches in diameter. Pour the raisin filling onto one-half of each circle, fold over the other half, and pinch it around the edges. Use enough filling to make each pie about ½ inch thick.

Fry the small pies in a hot Dutch oven, using enough cooking oil or fat to prevent them from sticking. Cook with the oven's lid on until the tops are brown. The same raisin mix can be used with a standard pie-crust mixture to bake regular pies on a tin plate in a Dutch oven.

Biscuits in a Flour Sack

My maternal grandfather hated to wash dishes. When my grandmother was sick, and he had to do the cooking, he taught us boys that a used dish became a dirty dish that had to be washed. To avoid this chore, he always mixed his biscuits in the top of a 50-pound sack of white flour.

After meticulously washing his hands, Grandpa would soberly tell us, "Always leave a little clean dirt on your hands, to mix off into the bread. It improves the flavor."

That is how I learned to mix biscuits in the top of a flour sack. The same procedure can be used at camp when a mixing pan is not available.

First, mix ½ cup of canned milk with ½ cup of cold water. Add 2 tablespoons of melted bacon fat and mix well. Smooth down the top part of the flour in a sack and make a small depression in the center. If the sack is only partly full, roll down the sides until the level of the flour is about 2 inches from the top of the sack. Into this depression, sprinkle ½ teaspoonful of salt and 2 level teaspoonfuls of baking powder. Then pour a little milk-water mixture into the depression. Mix in the flour, either with a spoon or by folding small amounts of flour over the liquid and mixing it together. Add more of the milk and water, mixing it with the flour. Keep the mixture stiff, not liquid. With care, all the liquid can be mixed with flour until a stiff dough remains. Knead the dough into a ball, and pinch off small portions which will become biscuit-sized when baked.

Bullburgers

One of the best ways to use lesser cuts of elk, deer, moose, or caribou meat is to make them into bullburgers. This allows you to use all parts of the animal without waste. You'll need a small food chopper, with a medium-coarse blade, for grinding the meat. The burgers will be better if the meat is ground twice.

Bullburgers may be made at camp, or at home from meat that has been frozen. Before grinding meat into burgers, allow it to cool thoroughly for several days. Tough, old bull animals should age from ten to fourteen days to break down the fibers of the meat.

When making burgers at camp, select cuts to be chopped on the basis of how fast they age. Rib and brisket cuts age quicker than the loins, hams, and shoulders. If the burgers are to be used immediately, it is all right to include areas of fat. However, if the meat patties are to be frozen, it is best to cut out most of the fat and substitute fat pork. Deer fat especially tends to become rancid with age when frozen. If you send your game to a processing plant, tell them to double-grind the meat and add 25 percent fat pork.

The simplest recipe for wild-game bullburger is to mix the ground meat with sliced or diced onions, shape it into flat patties nearly half-inch thick, and fry in a heavy skillet, on a heavy griddle, or in a Dutch oven. Serve on heated, buttered buns or toast, or as part of a regular meal, with a few slices of dill pickle and catsup.

Bullburger can be used in a variety of combinations. The meat can be formed into small, round patties (1½ inches diameter). Prefry the patties and add them to nearly cooked macaroni. Another fine recipe, suitable for camp or home, requires large green peppers, one per person. Hollow out the peppers and slice them in half, lengthwise. Boil in enough water to cover for 20 minutes. While the peppers are boiling, fry small burgers, about the size of the pepper halves, mixed with diced or sliced onions. Salt and pepper the burgers before frying. When both peppers and patties are done, mix a tablespoonful of flour into the fat remaining from frying the burgers, and stir until it browns. Add the water in which the peppers were boiled, stirring constantly, and thicken into a sauce. Place a slice of bread or toast on each plate, add the sauce and a half pepper, open side up. Put a patty inside each pepper half, add sauce, and serve.

To combine bullburgers and chile, follow this recipe. Break half a pound of burger into small pieces with a fork, and fry in a skillet. When browned, salt lightly, then add a 16-ounce can of prepared chili con carne and mix with the meat. Heat to near boiling. Add water as it cooks to give the desired consistency. If thin, eat in a bowl with crackers or bread. If thick, spread over toast or buns.

For a hot lunch that is quickly prepared and nourishing, try Mexican burgers. Ingredients needed are:

½ cup chopped onion
⅓ cup chopped peppers
½ pound bullburger
6-ounce can of tomato paste
½ cup water
1¼ teaspoonfuls salt,
   pinch of pepper, or to taste
1-2 teaspoonfuls chili powder
1 small can of pork and beans

Break the bullburger into small pieces with a fork and sauté in a skillet, with the chopped peppers and onion, until brown. Stir the tomato paste into the half cup of water and add to the meat. Add salt, pepper, and chili. Finally, add pork and beans, stir well, and heat until piping hot. Serve over buttered toast with fresh salad or fruit.

How to Cook Tongue

One of the best cuts of meat from a big-game animal, the tongue, is often left behind in the woods. The tongue of elk and moose is especially good, and of considerable size. It is easily removed, after the animal's head has been detached, by cutting up from the throat area and freeing the tongue from its base.

To prepare tongue, wash it and then boil it for two or three hours in salted water (1 tablespoonful salt to the gallon). After boiling, peel off the skin with a sharp knife. The meat can be thinly sliced and used for sandwiches. Deer tongue is prepared in the same way.

Cooking Sheep Ribs on an Open Fire

The meat of wild sheep is among the most delicious of all game meat. Of the various cuts, none surpasses the ribs, especially when cooked over an open fire. I watched a Tahltan Indian hunter cook sheep ribs in this way, his only utensil a length of green spruce.

He built a roaring fire and allowed it to burn down to coals which gave off a regular heat. Meanwhile he prepared the large slab of ribs by paring down the loin area so that it equaled the thickness of the rib area and would cook evenly. He found a length of green spruce and sharpened both ends, shoved one end into the ground, about a foot from the edge of the fire and slanted slightly toward it.

He impaled the ribs on the stake at the center, a bit toward the top, with the outside toward the fire. Almost at once, the meat began to bubble as the fat melted. As the meat cooked, the fat basted it and kept it from burning. The Indian regulated the heat by moving the coals of the fire. When they died down, he put on a little dry kindling. He turned the ribs when they were done on one side.

After an hour or so, the meat was ready. He pulled the stake from the ground, sliced off a rib for each of us, and salted them. We ate the ribs with our hands, like corn on the cob. I've seldom eaten better meat.

Later the Indian told me that when a hunter of his tribe had to travel long distances in wilderness country, he carried only a rifle, a small rucksack, and some salt. When he killed an animal, he used the ribs first, cooking them the way he had shown me. He put the remains in the rucksack, and ate some for lunch the next day. The following day he would dry, smoke, and cut the rest of the meat into long slices. Packing as much meat as possible in his small rucksack, the hunter would continue his journey, and when the meat was nearly gone, he would kill another animal. The Indian told me that he'd once crossed most of British Columbia with only a rifle, a rucksack, and some salt.

Moose Nose

Among the Indians of the North the cooked nose of a moose has long been considered a delicacy, for the long bulbous section, from the end of the septum to the tip, contains considerable meat. The entire nose was chopped or sawed off, coated with mud, and placed in a bed of hot coals. After several hours it would be completely cooked. When the caked mud was removed, most of the hair would come off and the rest could be scraped away. The meat was separated from the bone, salted, and eaten. Moose nose may still be prepared this way in a hunting camp.

A more sophisticated way of cooking moose nose is to boil it. The entire nose section, including the lower part of the upper jawbone, may be used, or only the bulbous nose area. First parboil the nose in a large kettle for forty-five minutes. Then remove it and place in a container of cold water to cool.

When the nose has cooled, pick off the hair. Immerse the nose in sufficient fresh, cold water to cover it. Add a couple of onions, a clove of garlic, and a tablespoonful of salt. Allow to simmer until tender, and then leave overnight in the same liquid. In the morning, the white meat of the bulbous section may be thinly sliced and used for sandwiches or snacks. If desired, elk tongue and moose nose may be pickled in vinegar.

Eskimo Steak

In the winter of 1959, while I was hunting in the Arctic, an Eskimo hunter named Ookeelah (which means Run Fast) showed me how to prepare Eskimo steak.

Inside his tiny igloo he thawed out some pieces of fresh caribou meat which he'd brought from his little village of Point Hope, Alaska. The meat was from the animal's brisket area and contained fat marbling. When it was thawed, Ookeelah cut it into ¾-inch cubes. He boiled these tiny cubes of raw meat in a pot on the puny gas stove he used to heat tea water when traveling. He used chunks of ice from a nearby lake for water. He added a couple of pinches of salt to the boiling water.

When the meat had boiled for nearly a half-hour, Ookeelah set the pot on the table. Then he heated some seal oil he'd rendered from the blubber of a hair seal and poured it into a tin cup.

We ate the meat by impaling a cube on a fork and dipping it into the warm seal oil. He called this "Eskimo steak" and told me soberly that his people had to eat it or else they would get sick. Living in that harsh land, and lacking green vegetables and other sources of vitamins, the Eskimos had discovered that the oil of the seal compensated for their vitamin deficiency. They ate only the brisket and ribs of the inland caribou they occasionally shot—the meat containing fat. In his broken English, Ookeelah assured me that the hams of the caribou were "—for dogs and good white-man food."

Potatoes and Onions in Foil

Easily prepared at camp with a minimum of utensils, this combination of potatoes and onions cooked in butter is often called German-fried spuds.

To prepare, peel the potatoes and slice thinly. Mix with peeled, sliced onions. A good ratio, if you like onions, is 1 onion to 3 potatoes. Add salt, pepper, and butter—about 1 tablespoonful of butter to each pint of potatoes and onions, mixed well.

Shape the mixture into a small rectangular loaf and wrap in foil. Cover lightly with hot coals. A quart-sized loaf should cook between twenty and thirty minutes.

If a small charcoal grill is available, the potatoes may be cooked on it. Wrap in two layers of foil to prevent the package from breaking open during handling. The layers should be folded on opposite sides. Turn once, when half cooked. It is often possible to tell when the potatoes are done by smelling the steam escaping from the folds.

Bullburgers, wieners, or pork chops go well with German-fried spuds.

Corn in Mud or Foil

To roast ears of sweet corn in an open fire, leave on the husks, smear them with thick mud, and bury them in a bed of hot coals. The mud cakes, holding in the moisture and flavor much as in pressure-cooking, and prevents burning. After approximately twenty minutes, remove the ears from the coals and strip off the caked mud and husks. Eat on the cob with butter and salt.

Roasting ears may also be wrapped in foil and cooked in hot coals. Again, the husks should be left on. Cooking time will be about twenty minutes, depending on the thickness of the husks and the size of the ears.

If roasting ears of corn are picked from a garden or purchased from farmers along the road, do not peel away the outer husks as is often done in supermarkets. With the green husks intact, the ears can be roasted in hot coals without first covering them with mud or foil.

Small wire
or wet cord

Tie husk ends before roasting corn in hot coals.

The trick is to gether all the husk ends together over the tip of the ear and tie them with a short length of thin wire or a wet cord. The wet cord will burn through during the cooking, but it will hold the husk ends over the end of the cob long enough to prevent burning. Tying the husks keeps the steam in while the corn is roasting. Ears of sweet corn cooked in this way don't have the swampy taste imparted by certain types of mud. And corn roasted in any manner retains its garden flavor better than corn boiled in water.

Making Jerky

The American Indians, through necessity, made a great contribution to the process of preserving fresh meat. Their problem was three-fold. First, fresh meat was a main part of their diet, and game animals were normally killed at considerable distances from their villages. Second, it was hard during summer season to use up an entire animal before spoilage set in. Third, on their travels they needed a food which was light but sustaining, and could be carried.

The Indians solved all three problems by cutting meat into long strips and drying it in the sun. Smoke, and salt when available, were used in the curing process to some extent.

Indians of the North country still jerk much of their fresh meat. Within the past decade I have been in the Alaska bush and seen Indian hunters kill a moose. They would camp for several days while they cut the meat into long strips, hang it from drying racks made of willow and alder, and cure it in the sun, keeping a slow birch fire going beneath it. While traveling down the Yukon River, between Dawson and Eagle, Alaska, I photographed the long drying racks where literally hundreds of king salmon, taken from the fish-wheels of the river, had been hung in strips and were being smoke-dried. Again, at a hunting camp at Beaver Creek, Alaska, the part-Indian female cook made moose jerky from the trophy bull I had shot, and it was delicious.

Many hunters like to make venison or antelope meat into jerky. Not only does it add variety to the camp menu, but is a palatable and sustaining meat for lunches and snacks.

There are dozens of recipes for making jerky, but

they all require drying the fresh meat before spoilage can occur. How thick and wide the strips of meat are cut is determined to some extent by the season. If it is sunny when the drying process begins, the strips are cut larger than they would be in wet weather.

Here is a basic recipe for deer or antelope jerky. It is very simple, and a good one for the beginner:

Cut the meat, preferably ham or shoulder, into long strips 1-inch wide and ¼-inch thick. Cut with the grain. Pare off all fat, as it will turn rancid in jerky.

Next, lay the strips on a breadboard or other flat board, and sprinkle them generously on both sides with black pepper. Use approximately twice as much as for steak or chops. Rub the pepper well into the meat with the hands. When this is done, thread a length of white cotton cord through the end of each piece of meat, using a large darning needle. The cord is for hanging the strip.

Fill a 5-gallon can with water and bring to a boil. Blanch the strips of meat in the boiling water by immersing each piece for ten seconds, removing it, and immersing it for another ten seconds.

Lightly brush each piece with prepared liquid smoke. Then hang the strips to dry. In an arid climate, they may be hung on a line in a cool, dry room where it will take from eight to ten days to dry. The strips also may be hung from a pole outside in the sunshine, protected from flies by a cheesecloth "tent," and high enough so dogs can't get at them. It should take three or four days for the meat to dry. Store the dried meat in cloth bags, preferably hung off the ground, or in cold storage.

Other recipes differ largely in the mixture of spices and how they are applied to the meat and the size of the strips.

The curing salt may be applied directly to strips, instead of blanching them in boiling salt water. Curing salt can be obtained from a processing plant. Rub the salt thoroughly into the strips and leave them in a cool place overnight before hanging them to dry. You can make your own curing salt from 1 pound of salt, 6 ounces of Prague powder, 2½ ounces of sugar, and 1 ounce of white pepper, all mixed thoroughly. For those who like jerky very hot, 1 ounce of cayenne pepper may be added. This mixture is sufficient for 40 to 50 pounds of fresh meat.

If damp weather is a problem, or if your patience is limited, the drying process may be speeded up by putting the thin strips into pans so they do not touch and slowly drying them in a warm, but not hot, oven. The oven temperature should be between 100 and 150 degrees, and the strips should be turned occasionally. Drying also may be speeded by putting the strips in a meat smoker which has a low heat output.

For the person who wants to make jerky at home, and can use an electric oven, here is a fine recipe:

Cut strips of lean meat (deer, antelope, elk, or beef) ⅛ inch thick and lay them in a dripping pan or small dish pan. Sprinkle the first layer with a good brand of seasoning salt, as you would salt a steak. Put one drop of liquid smoke onto each strip and brush it evenly with a pastry brush. Pepper the strips with seasoning pepper, and sprinkle them again with a light coating of granulated sugar. If you like garlic, sprinkle the strips lightly with garlic salt. Line the pan with a second layer and add the seasoning. Continue adding layers of strips, seasoning each layer until the pan is nearly full or the meat runs out. Let the pan of meat set from five to seven hours. For tough meat, overnight is not too long.

Get as many oven shelves as possible—one for each bracket is desirable. Take each shelf out of the oven, cover it with the prepared strips, and replace it. Set the temperature for 100 degrees, and heat the strips from six to seven hours. Strips cut thicker than ⅛ inch may take longer. When the strips are dried brittle, the jerky will be done. It may then be stored indefinitely in cloth, paper, or plastic bags, in the home freezer or refrigerator.

Neck Stew

This is a hearty camp recipe for big-game hunters in elk country. A day after an elk has been killed and cooled, chop 2 pounds of meat from the neck just behind the ears, using a clean ax. Chop the meat into chunks approximately one-third the size of a clenched fist, including a little bone. Wash the chunks and put them in a large kettle or Dutch oven, cover with water, and simmer for about two hours. After the contents of the kettle have been "skimmed," add 6 sliced carrots and allow to simmer for thirty minutes. Then add 1 large onion, sliced, 1 small head of cabbage cut into chunks about 1½ inches thick, and 2 small potatoes, quartered. Simmered for about thirty minutes, then add a few bay leaves, and salt and pepper to taste. Add water as needed. Ten minutes before serving, add a medium-sized can of condensed tomato soup. If tomato soup is not available, ¼ small bottle of catsup may be used. Bring to a simmer and serve. This recipe will make a gallon of stew.

Venison Chili

Exceptionally fine venison chili can be made at

camp, if preparation is made in advance and a few necessary items brought along. The ingredients needed are as follows:

> 2 pounds ground or diced venison
> ⅓ cup diced onions
> ¼ teaspoonful minced garlic
> 2 teaspoonfuls ground cumin
> 3 tablespoonfuls flour
> 1 teaspoonful salt
> ¼ teaspoonful pepper
> 2½ cups tomato juice
> 2 tablespoonfuls chili powder

The venison may be diced by cutting it into ¼-inch cubes with a sharp knife on a flat board, or it may be run through a small food grinder.

Sauté cubed or ground meat, with the onions and garlic, in a Dutch oven, for about fifteen minutes, stirring occasionally. Add cumin, chili powder, flour, salt, pepper, and stir. Then add the tomato juice. Cover and cook for another fifteen minutes, uncover and cook for fifteen minutes more.

Serve hot over preheated chili beans. This recipe serves eight people.

If deer meat is not available, elk, moose, or caribou may be substituted. Venison is best, however, owing to its finer texture.

This same recipe may be used at home to prepare chili in bulk for freezing. After preparing the chili mixture, allow it to cool thoroughly and put it in pint-sized plastic refrigerator bags. Tie the bags shut and put in the freezer. Chili made in this way should be used within a six-month period.

Tenderloin

Hunters usually quarter their elk before packing it into camp. In the process, the tenderloins are often cut up and sometimes damaged. The tenderloins are among the best cuts, and should be pared away before the carcass is cut into quarters.

This choice cut should be cooled overnight then sautéd in hot butter in a heavy skillet or Dutch oven. To prepare for the pan, cut the tenderloin into sections approximately 1 inch thick. Heat ⅛ pound of butter in the skillet until it sizzles, then put in the pieces of meat. Semisear on one side, turn and semisear the opposite side. Set the skillet over a slower heat and cook for several minutes until done to taste. Salt and pepper before serving.

Beans and Ham Hocks

One of the best camp meals, especially in cold weather, is a mixture of dry beans and ham hocks. The following recipe serves three people.

Wash 1½ pints of dry, white beans, place in a large pot, and cover with 2 inches of water. Place on the fire and allow to simmer, adding water as required so the beans do not cook dry.

Cut ham hock which still contains some meat into small chunks and add to the beans after they have simmered for three hours. Add salt, pepper, and a dash of catsup. Simmer for another hour and serve with buttered bread and fresh fruit.

Camp Coffee or Tea

Most outdoorsmen drink a lot of coffee, and can

make a good cup with the home percolator or drip coffeepot. Some don't do so well over a campfire.

Camp coffee is best when made in an enameled coffeepot. However, it can be made in an aluminum pot, a kettle, or even in a Dutch oven. Some of the best camp coffee ever made has been brewed in a 2-pound coffee can rigged with a wire bail.

Use regular-grind coffee, one heaping teaspoonful to each cup of water. Those who like their coffee strong add an extra spoonful "for the pot." Fill the pot with the required number of cups of cold water and set on the coals to heat. As the water heats, add the equivalent number of spoonfuls of coffee.

The coffee grounds will stay on the water's surface as the water heats, and will "grow" as the water reaches the boiling point. The coffee must be watched carefully at this stage or else it will boil over. If you're using a coffee can, lay a green alder across the top. It will dampen the rolling boil as the water reaches the top.

When the water boils, allow the grounds to settle and mix with the boiling water for approximately thirty seconds, then take the pot off the coals to let the coffee settle, or brew. Set the pot just far enough away from the heat so that it will remain hot but not simmer. In five minutes, the coffee will be ready to pour. If it hasn't completely settled, add a dash of cold water.

Many outdoorsmen of the Far North prefer tea instead of coffee. They say it keeps them warmer on the trail. Tea can be made at camp in an enameled teapot, an aluminum pot, or a metal tea pail used by many Canadian woodsmen. The pot used for making tea should not be used for making coffee.

Do not boil tea. Heat the water to the boiling point, add the tea leaves, and remove the pot from the fire to steep. An average mixture is one level teaspoonful of tea leaves for each cup of water. The steeping time depends on individual taste, but after about three minutes tea will become bitter. If an earthenware pot is available, first put in the tea and then add boiling water for a couple of minutes.

Tea bags are very handy for making camp tea, but the quality of the tea in bags is generally poorer than that sold in bulk. Many campers like black tea, others prefer green. Canadians and Alaskans have developed a taste for the wild Hudson Bay tea, often called Labrador tea or mountain tea. This grows wild on small bushes having rosette-shaped leaves. These green, waxy leaves will give off a delicate odor similar to eucalyptus. This is one way of identifying the plant. It is found in the northern tier of the states near the Canadian border, in Canada, and in much of Alaska. Fur traders used it to supplement their supply of regular tea, and some later came to use it exclusively.

To make Hudson Bay tea for two people, pick about a dozen leaves and boil them in water for three minutes. (It takes time for the hard leaves to give up their flavor.) Then remove the leaves from the water and bring it to a boil. Combine the Hudson Bay tea with a little black tea and you'll have a delicious, warming drink.

Hudson Bay tea leaves may be picked and dried, and taken along for future use. The best way to dry the leaves is to place them in a brown paper bag near the camp stove. A quart dries in a few hours and weighs very little.

Making Hotcake Syrup

Occasionally at camp the syrup runs out before the hotcakes. Rather than disappoint hungry campers, make your own syrup of sugar and water. Just pour a cupful of granulated white sugar into a heavy skillet and place the skillet over the fire. Stir the sugar until it is an even brown. Add a cup of boiling water and stir vigorously until the sugar is dissolved. Do not allow the sugar to burn or turn black. The result is a tasty syrup that blends well with hotcakes. If a little maple flavoring is available, a half teaspoonful will improve the taste of the syrup.

Tin Can Chowder

A tasty chowder can be made at camp from surplus fish. A large tin can, or several small ones, serves as a cooking pot, though a Dutch oven is best. The ingredients needed are:

2 cups shredded fish
1 cup diced potatoes
1 small diced onion
½ cup diced celery stalks
4 slices thin bacon diced, or salt pork if available
½ cup canned milk
Salt and pepper

If fish from a fish-fry are left over, these may be used. Otherwise, fresh fish should be boiled for seven minutes in a clean cloth. The flesh can then be picked from the bones.

Brown the bacon in the can or oven, then add the onion and cook over low heat until partly done. Add potatoes, celery, and two cups of water (this may be the water used for boiling the fish). Salt to taste. Allow to simmer until the vegetables are tender, then add the fish and milk. Pepper to taste, heat to near boiling, and serve.

Steamed Clams

Outdoorsmen who travel along ocean beaches often find clam beds that yield a couple of bushels. If you've dug soft shell clams, you can steam them at camp with only a large bucket and a piece of large-mesh screen.

Cut a circle from the screen having a diameter just 8 inches larger than the diameter of the bucket at a point 4 inches from the bottom. Then cut the circular screen in spokelike segments, as shown in the drawing. Bend in the segments to form a small basket. Place this basket, rim down, into the bucket. The flat part of the screen will now be 4 inches from the bottom of the bucket.

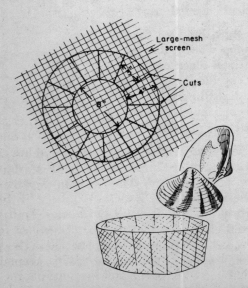

Pattern for cutting steaming basket, top, and finished basket, which is placed in bucket rim down.

Fill the bucket with about 2 inches of water and set on the fire or stove to boil. Place the washed clams inside, on the screen, and put on the lid. The water is kept at a rolling boil, but does not touch the clams; the steam from the water cooks them. The clams will open in several minutes. They are done, ready to eat off the shell. Serve with buttered garlic bread.

Fillet of Tuotuava

When the tuotuava, or white sea bass, are running in southern waters fishermen usually fillet their catch and bring it home on ice in a cooler. The fish often weigh over a hundred pounds, and filleting is the best way to handle them.

Campers can enjoy a superb fish meal on the beach if they prepare for it in advance.

The big fish are skinned and filleted. The fillets to take home may be cut larger; those to be cooked on the beach are cut about 3 inches long by ½-inch wide and just under ½-inch thick.

Prepare a batter of cornflake crumbs, fresh egg, canned milk, a product called Dixie Fry, and the product Bisquick. The proportions of this batter are entirely flexible. The best way is to mix one beaten egg with a full cup of canned milk, then add equal parts of the other three ingredients until a thick batter is formed.

Dip the fillets into this batter, then deep-fry them in cooking oil. A large Dutch oven is excellent for this purpose. Fill it with about 2 inches of oil. The screen device suggested for steaming clams is adaptable to frying fillets. Use it as a basket for lowering the fillets into the oil. Cooking time is approximately fifteen minutes, or until the fillets are golden brown.

Serve with fresh homemade bread, hot if possible, and spread with garlic butter. Lacking homemade bread, serve stone-ground bread, cut into slices 1½ inches thick, heated in a reflector oven or a Dutch oven, and generously spread with melted butter.

Sturgeon Sticks

Many people consider the great white sturgeon to be the best of all table fish. The best way to cook sturgeon is to cut it into fillets and fry them in butter.

When skinning the sturgeon, note that the flesh is mostly white, with intermittent skeins of reddish flesh. These red "strings" are the equivalent of fat and should be removed after the fillets are cut.

To cut the fillets, begin at the neck (after removing the head) and make a cut across the fish just 4 inches in length. The white sturgeon has no real backbone—just a notocord inside heavy cartilage. Cut 4-inch slices from either side of the fish along its entire length. Then cut these slices into sticks about 4 inches long, ¾ inch wide, and ½ inch thick.

Slowly fry the sticks in butter in a heavy skillet. Use enough butter to completely cover the skillet's bottom, and heat until it sizzles before putting in the sticks. Cook about forty minutes, or until golden brown, turning occasionally.

Cooking Fish Without Utensils

The go-light backpacker often needs to cook fish without utensils. Here's how to do it:

The fish should first be cut into fillets. Girdle the flesh just ahead of the tail and behind the gills and pectoral fins. Make longitudinal cuts on either side of the backbone and just above the belly line. Skin the fish by grasping a bit of skin raised by the incisions and peeling it away. A small pair of pliers is useful for this operation. When both sides are skinned, insert the thin blade of a knife between the flesh at the back and the ribs, and working downward, cut away the fillets.

One way to cook the fillets is to salt them, impale them on a green stick and toast them over the fire until they are cooked on both sides, taking care that they don't crumble and drop off the stick when they are nearly done. It is always best, of course, to let an open fire die down to a bed of coals before using it for cooking.

Another way to cook the fillets is to place a flat rock in the bottom of the fire pit when building the fire. After the fire has burned down to a bed of coals, scrape them away, exposing the red-hot rock. Flatten a tin can by cutting out both ends with a pocketknife and lay it on the rock. A fillet can then be cooked on the flat tin. Lacking a tin can, cover the rock with tinfoil or cook the fillet right on the rock itself.

Indians used to cook fish on a spit over an open fire. They would thrust a green stick completely

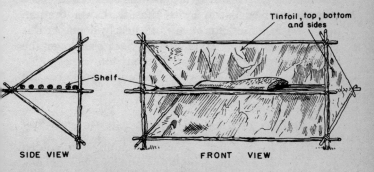

Reflector oven for baking fish.

through the fish, from mouth to tail, and suspend it over the fire on two forked sticks. As the fish cooked, it was rotated until done.

To bake fish, you can make a reflector oven with a few green sticks, some tinfoil, and a few nails or wire. First make the sides of the oven by nailing or wiring three short willows in the form of a triangle. Fasten crosspieces to these sides to form the oven, as shown in the drawing. A shelf of green sticks supports the fish. Cover all inside surfaces, except the shelf, with tinfoil. Set the oven in front of a bed of hot coals, with the fish on the shelf. The reflected heat bakes the fish.

Small fish may be salted and baked whole. Larger fish should be cut into fillets, with the skin left on, and baked with the skin side next to the shelf. The skin prevents the fish from crumbling and falling through the gaps in the shelf.

Baked Lake Trout

Here is a recipe for trout that are too large to cook in a skillet. First stuff the trout with a dressing like that used for turkey. Lay it on its side in a baking pan and spoon a row of dressing around the fish. Then place strips of smoked bacon across the fish. Cover the pan and bake in a medium oven until nearly done. At this point, pour a can of condensed tomato soup over the fish and bake until the soup thickens into a paste. To serve, cut the fish crosswise into ample portions and add dressing.

Golden Trout

If you're ever lucky enough to catch some golden trout around 12 inches long, this is the best way to cook them.

To cook two or three fish, heat ⅛ pound of butter in a Dutch oven until it sizzles. Salt the fish lightly and place in the hot oven. Fry about two minutes on each side.

Crumbed Trout

One of the finest ways to cook medium-size trout is to skin them, dip them into a batter of bread or cracker crumbs mixed with buttermilk, then fry them to a golden brown in hot butter.

Fish in Foil

This is a simple way to cook pan-sized fish, especially trout, and preserve the flavor and moisture of the fish.

Clean the fish, then salt and pepper lightly, and coat with butter inside and out. For a 12-inch trout, use about 1 tablespoonful of butter. Wrap each fish individually in a layer of aluminum foil, folding the edges of the foil tightly, otherwise as the butter melts it will escape.

Allow the cooking fire to die down to a bed of hot coals, and rake them over the foil-covered fish. Allow to cook without disturbance. Cooking time depends on the size of the fish and the quality of the coals. For a pine-wood fire, and a 12-inch trout, the cooking time is just twenty minutes. To serve, simply open the foil and use it as a plate on which to eat the fish.

Pan-sized fish may be wrapped in foil and cooked on a grill over charcoal. Turn once, after approximately three-fourths of the cooking time has elapsed. Part of the butter will be lost from leakage, but this won't affect the taste of the fish.

Smoking Fish

In wilderness country where the fish are coopera-
tive, often more are caught than can be eaten at camp.
Rather than waste extra fish, you may want to preserve
them and take them home. Smoking them is the answer.

We once found a smokehouse in British Columbia
which Indians had built and abandoned, and used it
for smoking our catch. Slender aspen poles had been
formed into a small wigwam about 4 feet high and
covered with sheets of green bark from the larger trees,
leaving a tiny aperture at the top. A small pit for the
fire had been dug just inside the bark covering. The
draft was regulated by moving the sheets of bark. The
fish were placed on a small platform of green alders
near the top. The only flaw in this smokehouse was
that, unless you were careful, the bark covering would
catch fire and burn up the entire outfit.

A better smokehouse can be made by using a canvas tarp for a covering. Build the platform about 3 feet
high by driving four green alder poles into the ground
and wiring or nailing crossbars at the tops and a few
inches down. Lay green alder sticks across these crossbars to form platforms. Build the fire just inside the
front of this framework, preferably in a shallow pit that
extends outside the house, into which the fuel can be
fed.

With the fire started, and the fish on the alder
shelves, wrap the canvas around the framework, leaving only a small opening at the top. This allows enough
upward draft to keep the smoke coming up through
the house so the fire will not die out.

With two lengths of stovepipe and a cardboard
carton about 2 feet square, you can build another type

of smokehouse that is even better. Find a cutbank about 4 feet high, and from the shoreline of a lake or stream. At the edge of the cutbank build a small framework of willows or alders similar to the one just described. The carton should fit over the top of the framework. Cut a small door 4 inches square in the bottom of the carton for a draft. Leave one side of the door uncut so it can be bent open and shut.

Next build a small cairn of rocks, sod, or dirt on the shoreline, two stovepipe lengths from the smokehouse. Lay the stovepipe between an opening in the top rear of the cairn and the interior of the smokehouse. Cover the pipe with dirt or support it with rocks to keep it in place.

Build a small fire in the cairn and add green alder or aspen wood to make it smoke. Regulate the smoke by placing a piece of tinfoil, a tin plate, or a sheet of metal cut from a large tin can on top of the fire. The smoke travels up to the smokehouse and smokes the fish without danger of burning them by a sudden blaze of fire.

For smoking fish at home, make the smokehouse out of a 50-gallon oil drum. Cut out both ends. At a point about 6 inches from the end that will be the top, run three small iron rods through the barrel through holes cold-chiseled in the sides. Onto these lay a small wire grate (the shelf from an electric oven). Place a few green willows across the top of the barrel, and on top of these lay one of the cut-out ends. This will keep most of the smoke inside the drum, but allow enough draft for the smoke to rise through the barrel. Place the fish on the wire grate.

Dig a shallow pit just inside the rim of the barrel, and build a small fire, adding green wood to make it smoke.

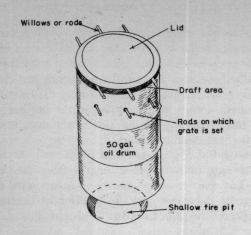

Willows or rods

Lid

Draft area

Rods on which
grate is set

50 gal.
oil drum

Shallow fire pit

Smokehouse made from oil drum.

Prepare fish for smoking by soaking them overnight in a strong solution of salt water. This drains the blood and seasons the fish. Small fish, such as 1-pound trout, should be smoked about seven hours. When the fish are deep brown and wrinkled they are done.

The best wood for smoking fish is apple wood. Often an angler near some rancher's orchard can arrange to save the prunings from spring orchard work, take them home, and use them for smoking up a batch of spring-caught trout. In the hills, the best wood is green aspen splits. Both apple and aspen impart a fine flavor to smoked fish.

Finally, here's a more sophisticated smokehouse you can build in your backyard from an old refrigerator. The shelves for holding the fish already exist.

Obtain a small one-burner hotplate. Take out enough of the seal around the refrigerator door to admit an electric cord, and put the hotplate inside the refrigerator on the bottom. Place a shallow metal pie-tin filled with hardwood sawdust on the hotplate. Shut the refrigerator door and turn on the hotplate. The fish will be smoked. If there isn't enough draft, remove more of the door seal. The hardwood sawdust must burn without flaming. Regulate the amount of air entering the refrigerator, or shift the tin on the hotplate, to produce the right amount of smoke.

This lazy man's smoker can preserve fish in half the time it takes an outside smokehouse, for all the smoke is condensed and used. Hardwood sawdust can be obtained from furniture manufacturers.

PART 5

Hiking and Backpacking How-To

How Far to Travel

Hiking and backpacking are gaining in popularity. There is no better exercise than walking, and when combined with fishing, hunting, rock collecting, or photography, hiking trips are a healthful and rewarding activity.

The basic problem for beginners is planning their first trips according to their physical limitations. Many live in urban areas where there is little opportunity to do much hiking or backpacking. When the time comes to take an extended hike in the country, they are apt to overdo it, simply because of overeagerness. The solution, of course, is to take it easy on the first outings, lest overexertion cause illness or worse.

A good approach to the problem is to consider the capabilities of young, well-conditioned hikers and make the necessary adjustments to your own age and conditioning.

For example, a Marine toughened by boot-camp training is expected to hike 50 miles in 24 hours.

Boy Scouts train with a series of hikes starting at 5 miles, progressing to 10, 25, and finally 50. Last summer, my grandson, age 12, and 17 other boys, attempted the 50-mile hike. They had taken the 5- and 10-mile hikes, but skipped the 25-miler. They did not carry packs and had 20 hours to complete the hike. Several trucks tagged along to pick up anyone who dropped out. Every boy completed the hike under the 20-hour limit. My grandson and a 14-year-old boy, to add a youthful flourish to the affair, sprinted the final 200 yards to see who could outrun the other. All these boys were farm-raised and exceptionally fit. Scoutmasters have told me that a 16-year-old boy in good physical condition can carry a 25-pound pack, if it fits well, and take extended overnight hikes without undue effort.

The average mountain man or professional outdoorsman can backpack a load of around 35 pounds for a considerable distance in gentle hill country without too much effort. I have carried 60 pounds on a packboard. And several times I've hiked 17 miles in the mountains in just over five hours.

These are examples of what young men, or men in top physical condition, can do. The average office worker in his thirties or forties should never even consider equaling these feats unless he has spent months conditioning himself. And since most people lack the time and inclination to embark on a fitness course, their first hikes should be short, their goals modest.

A good way for the average urbanite to plan a hike is to consider how far he has recently been able to walk without tiring. If he has walked a mile in the city without difficulty, then a mile hike or a bit more will be pleasant. If he has been bird hunting recently, and has carried a shotgun, shells, and birds for about 3 miles in an afternoon, then backpacking a 15- to 20-pound load for 3 miles won't prove too tiring.

Needless to say, the best way to train for a hiking trip is to walk as much as possible. Walking in preparation for an extended hike strengthens the muscles that will be used and gives a person the chance to gauge his endurance.

Setting a Pace

On a long hike, try to set as leisurely a pace as possible. Avoid hurrying the pace to reach a certain destination on time. Hurrying will only cause fatigue; a steady, relaxed pace conserves energy and actually covers more ground in the long run.

A lone hiker tends to set a comfortable pace for himself, but when two men hike together, one usually sets the pace and the other follows. If the pacesetter happens to be a fast walker, his partner will hurry his strides to keep up and tire quickly. If the pacesetter is a slow walker, the follower will check his normal stride, and this too can be tiring. The best system is for each man to keep to his own pace, the faster pausing occasionally to allow his partner to catch up.

Of course, terrain has a great bearing on pace. In steep country, shorten your step and slow your pace, taking a zigzag rather than a straightline route up a hill. Although you'll have to hike farther, the ground won't be as steep, and the pressure on the edges of your feet will be alternated. In crossing terrain strewn with down timber, it is less strenuous to step over a log than on it. Climb a short distance and take a rest, then continue until you feel in need of another rest. A good rule is to climb toward a point level with your eyes, rest, continue toward a second point, and so on.

Hiking Shoes

The most important item of clothing for hiking is a good pair of shoes. A poor-fitting pair will spoil any hike, and on an extended trek can cripple the feet.

Most shoes used for hiking have two faults. They are too heavy and they are uncomfortable. For serious hiking and especially for backpacking, shoes should be of the lightest weight consistent with high quality, and they should be relatively comfortable when you first try them.

Many shoes advertised for hiking won't fill these requirements. Some are 10 inches high, of heavy leather, and have heavy logger-type heels and cleated vibram soles. Such shoes are *rugged* enough for hiking in the mountains—the problem is trying to get them up there.

Hiking shoes should not be over 8 inches high. Six inches is better for most purposes. I have long advocated a compromise 7-inch height, but shoe manufacturers have been reluctant to make them.

Hiking shoes should be made of the finest, glove-soft leather; the best soles are a combination of cord and rubber or rubber synthetic. This material will wear much longer than pure crepe soles, and give better traction on rocks, wet grass, slippery logs, or shelving ledges than will leather soles. Leather soles are far too slippery for hiking. The heels should also be of cord-type construction, with a square-cut face, and ¾ to 1 inch high. Heels that slope backward at the front end or, worse, are integral with the sole so that the entire bottom surface of the shoe is flat do not hold the ground well and tend to slip off small projections.

Many shoes for sportsmen are of the pull-on type. These are fine for around camp, but are not good for hiking. They slip off the heel when climbing and cause blisters or roll up the socks. Hiking shoes should always be laced.

Leather cannot be completely waterproofed. One of the best preparations for treating shoes is a silicone compound which withstands moisture and temporary wetting. Though often advertised for waterproofing shoes, it will not withstand prolonged exposure to rain or wet snow.

Hiking shoes should not be entirely waterproof. They should be water-resistant, but should allow the feet to "breathe" as you walk. This prevents galling and excessive sweating of the feet, and is one of the reasons for wearing a low-cut shoe—air moves through the top at each step.

A hiking shoe should be a half-size larger than the shoe worn around the office or home. Feet swell under the strain of heavy walking, and this must be allowed for. If shoes are a trifle too large, wear an extra sock to take up the looseness and cushion the feet.

Never wear new shoes on a hike unless they have been broken in. The best way to break in new leather shoes is to put them on and stand in warm water for ten seconds, then allow them to dry on the feet. Even broken-in shoes should be worn for several days before a hike to be sure they are comfortable. To keep them in good condition, periodically apply a light coating of shoe grease such as Huber's or Pecard.

On hikes of several days, take along a pair of canvas sneakers to wear around camp in the morning and evening. Sneakers provide a change for the feet and give your hiking shoes a chance to dry and air. They are also useful for wading streams. The gravel in a stream bed often works under the socks and makes a pair of hiking shoes uncomfortable for hours after. With a pair of sneakers in your pack, you can change shoes to ford a stream, wash the socks and feet clean of sand and gravel, and again put on the hiking shoes. Moreover, if your leather hiking shoes are damaged during a hike, you'll have the sneakers to fall back on.

Leather shoes are adequate for hiking during spring, summer, and fall, when dry weather is the rule. During the winter, on wet ground or snow, or when using snowshoes, rubber-bottom pacs should be worn. The best height is 6 inches, the maximum 8. Wear a pair of lambskin innersoles and dry socks inside the pacs.

High, insulated rubber boots are not good for extensive hiking. They are airtight and do not permit the feet to "breathe." Feet become cold and clammy in such boots. Also, rubber boots are too heavy to wear on long hikes.

Packboards

Over the years, man has devised many methods of carrying loads. One of these is the tumpline, a band that goes around the forehead with ropes attached to each end. The ropes are tied to loads of various shapes and sizes which are packed on the back and supported by the neck muscles. The tumpline has been used extensively for hauling bulky objects for relatively short distances, such as on portages in canoe country. Another device for carrying loads is the packbasket, a large basket woven of reeds or slats, and carried on the back by means of a pair of shoulder straps. Knapsacks and rucksacks—canvas sacks with shoulder straps—have long been used for carrying light loads. The packbasket, knapsack, and rucksack all have the advantage of being able to carry small items. The packbasket has the added advantage of protecting the wearer's back against hard objects carried inside.

For heavy loads, however, no backpacking device surpasses a good packboard. The packboard is what its name suggests—a form of board equipped with shoulder straps to which a load can be lashed. The packboard, or packframe, is so designed that a canvas wrap or webbing instead of the load rides directly on the wearer's back. The load itself is usually separated from the wrap or webbing. This design permits the entire load to be distributed over an area of the back equivalent to the surface of the packboard.

One successful packboard of the past has been the Trapper Nelson. This consists of a frame, a wrap, shoulder straps, and a series of eye-screws on the outside of the frame to which a load is lashed. Odd-shaped loads are wrapped in a tarp, poncho, plastic sheet, or other covering and lashed to the board with a light rope running back and forth across the frame and through the eyelets, much as one laces a shoe.

A complement of the Trapper Nelson board is a rectangular packsack made of canvas. This sack has snaps which fasten to the eyelets of the frame and is used for carrying a load of small items. This eliminates the need for wrapping the entire cargo into a single bundle and lashing it directly to the board.

One of the most used packboards today is the military model developed during World War II. It consists of a molded fiber frame with hooks along its edges to which loads are lashed. Another combination packboard-packsack developed at the same time consists of a light metal A-frame to which a canvas, pocketed packsack is attached. The apex of the A-frame, which rests high between the shoulders, is padded with leather. The bulk of the load is kept off the small of the wearer's back by a heavy web strap held under tension between the sides of the metal frame.

Perhaps the best modern packboard for carrying heavy loads is the Himalayan type. This consists of a light tubular-aluminum frame equipped with a shoulder harness and with web straps that ride on the small of the back. A small shelf of aluminum tubing at the lower back keeps the load from sagging.

The key to easy packing lies in properly distributing the load. For hiking on level terrain, the heaviest part of the load should be placed high on the board. For climbing, a large part of the load should be placed lower down, just at the small of the back above the hips. Pack most of the weight and bulk nearest to the board. Keeping the center of gravity close to the body prevents the load from tipping backward.

Walking Stick from a Hoe

Ice often forms in low spots on a trail, and when covered with fresh snow these pose a hazard for the hiker. With a sharp-tipped walking stick made from an old garden hoe, you can punch into such spots and prevent a bad spill. In summer such a walking stick is useful for crossing streams.

Cut off the hoe where the shank joins the blade, using a hacksaw, torch, or grinder. Heat the shank in a forge, or even in an open fire, until it is hot. (With an open fire, be careful not to burn the handle where the shank enters the ferrule.) Straighten the heated shank by hammering it on an anvil, the flat side of an ax, or a large rock. Then sharpen the end with a grinder or file. Cut the handle to a comfortable length for your height.

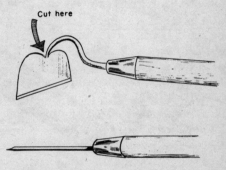

Sharp-pointed walking stick, made from a hoe, prevents spills when hiking on icy ground or when crossing streams.

The handle of an old hoe is often brittle and may split, so coat it lightly with linseed oil. In time, your hand will rub the oil into the wood and the handle won't sliver or crack unduly.

Walking Stick from a Sapling

A sharp-tipped walking stick can be quickly improvised in camp if you have a 16d spike, a length of small-gauge wire, and a short nail or flathead screw. Cut off the head of the spike by notching it on opposite sides with a file, then breaking it off with the claws of a hammer. Sharpen the spike slightly at this end. Find a dry sapling about 1 inch in diameter and 5 feet long, trim off the branches, and whip the larger end with the wire for about 1 inch. Finish the whipping by winding

Walking stick improvised from a spike and sapling.

the wire around the small nail or screw, which should be imbedded in the wood at the proper place, and then set flush. Finally, drive the spike into the end of the staff. The whipping will prevent the wood from splitting.

Grub List for Hiking

An adequate but light grub supply is very important to the backpacker. Every extra ounce becomes that much more of a burden on a long hike. Nevertheless, one hikes for enjoyment, and having enough to eat is part of the pleasure.

Meals for a backpacking trip are planned in exactly the same way as for any other type of expedition, and this has been explained in Part III, "Grub List." The basic consideration for a backpacking trip is to choose those foods containing the least amount of water. Springs and streams will supply the water lacking in the food. By using dehydrated, dried, or specially prepared foods, the normal water content can be reduced by 75 percent. As one example, a popular brand of prepared dry soup mix weighs 3½ ounces. When cooked in boiling water, it makes six 8-ounce servings, or a total of 48 ounces of soup.

In the cereal group, such items as cornflakes, premixed hotcake flour, dry rice, macaroni, hardtack, crackers, and pilot-biscuit all have relatively little water content and weigh very little. When prepared, they are filling and nourishing.

In the meat group, such items as bacon, (used both for food and for its grease for frying), chipped beef, salami, and jerky are all relatively light but nourishing. Fresh meat in the form of game animals or birds, or fish, should not be relied on. Numerous vegetables now come in dry or dehydrated form, or are available as dry packaged soups. These include such staples as beans, peas, carrots, and onions. Often the short protein of a limited meat, bread, or cheese menu can be augmented by these dry vegetable soups. Fruits such as apples, prunes, peaches, apricots, and grapes (raisins) also can be obtained in packaged, dehydrated form. On short trips, light, prepared dinners such as macaroni and cheese are adequate and require few utensils to cook.

Often when assembling foods for a backpacking trip, weight can be cut down by discarding the original can or carton and putting the food into plastic refrigerator bags. It is best to use two bags, one inside the other. The necks should be closed with a rubber band, or with one of the little covered-wire fasteners used by supermarkets. Be sure to include the instructions on the original package—just a few words written on a small piece of paper and placed in the plastic bag.

Food manufacturers have begun to cater more to the go-light outdoorsman and are marketing excellent condensed foods. Some of these are sold as individual items, from which you can make up your own grub list. Many, however, are sold as complete meals and menus. One popular brand is Perma-Pak. The foods may be bought as complete meals for a given number of people, and include a wide variety of breakfasts, lunches, and dinners.

This company makes up a three-day emergency food ration, packaged in the form of a belt containing several pockets which may be worn around the person like a money or cartridge belt. Refills are available to replace used items.

The old standby concentrated foods such as raisins, chocolate bars, pinole, and jerky are still useful today. Indian hunters discovered that they could travel and sustain themselves for many days at a time with only a bag of parched corn and some strips of jerky. I have hunted with Indians in the Far North and discovered that they know every edible wild fruit in the area and eat it steadily along the route. I could not induce one of these Indians to eat any canned fruit at our camp, but he ate gallons of wild blueberries, crow-berries, and cranberries as we traveled. When asked why canned peaches were not as good, he answered, "Can spoils them." One wild food usually neglected by the backpacker is watercress, which grows in many cold springs and creeks, and makes a nice salad with packaged foods.

PART 6

Photography How-To

Night Pictures

Most modern cameras are equipped to take flash pictures, and that is the simplest way to take outdoor pictures at night. Modern flashbulbs and flashcubes are not only inexpensive but very small for the amount of light they emit.

However, on backpacking or wilderness trips where every ounce counts, and flash equipment is excluded for reasons of portability, night pictures can be taken using only firelight. The fire should be allowed to burn down to a bed of coals to permit the subjects to stand close to it. When ready for the picture, toss a small armful of dry brush or twigs onto the coals so that the fire flares up. When the fire blazes up to the height of the subjects' knees, and their faces are illuminated, snap the picture. For black-and-white film with an ASA rating of 125, try an exposure of one second with the diaphragm set at f4.5, at a distance of 12 feet.

If you can seize the moment when dusk is falling, and the fading light of day can augment the firelight, an interesting photo can be taken. The light of the fire should be slightly stronger than the daylight. Test the light by squinting the eyes; the difference will then be readily apparent,

How to Make "Etchings"

Have you ever seen an attractive black-and-white picture in a magazine and wished to preserve it? If the picture has been printed on paper having a clay base, it can easily be transferred from the page to a piece of plywood. The result will resemble an old etching and will be an appropriate decoration for a wall in your home or vacation cabin.

In order to accomplish this transfer, obtain a product known as polymer medium from an art-supply store. This is sold under a variety of trade names. You'll also need a small brush.

To determine whether the magazine is printed on a paper with a clay base, wet a finger and run it over a page. If some of the coating comes off and has a chalky feel, the base is clay. Most coated paper used in "slick" magazines today has a clay base.

Cut the picture from the magazine and trim the margins. Then cut a piece of ¼-inch plywood to a size larger than the picture, leaving a suitable margin on all sides. Smooth the face and edges of the plywood with fine sandpaper. Dip the brush in water, and paint the face of the plywood with the polymer medium. Immediately place the picture face down on the plywood, being careful to put it exactly in position the first time as it is almost impossible to remove it once it contacts the polymer medium. (It's a good idea to rule corner marks for placement on the plywood.) With the picture in place, smooth it down with the back of a plastc comb, removing all air bubbles. Smooth from the center of the picture to the edges.

Allow the picture to dry for fifteen minutes. Then immerse the plywood board in a pan of warm water for a minute or two, until the paper is loosened and can be carefully peeled off. Allow the board to dry completely.

The picture will now be reproduced on the plywood, but in reverse. Just enough of the grain of the wood will show through to give the appearance of an old etching. Of course, copyright laws forbid anyone to use pictures in magazines for commercial purposes, so your "etchings" should be only for your own enjoyment.

Rustic Picture Frames

An outstanding photo deserves to be enlarged, and will be further enhanced by an attractive, rustic frame. If you are at all handy with tools, it is satisfying to make your own frames for your favorite outdoor photos.

The best wood for making rustic frames is pine, spruce, or fir. Select a straight, dry sapling or branch about 2 inches in diameter with just a trace of green in it. If the wood is slightly green, the bark will remain on the frame longer. The pole need only be long enough to cut two sides of the frame, since it will be split in half and both halves used. When determining the length, be sure to figure the outside dimensions of the frame, to allow for the mitered corners.

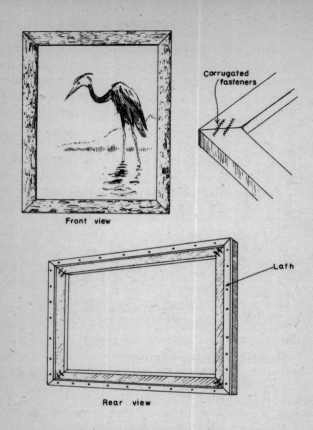

Corrugated fasteners

Front view

Lath

Rear view

Chipped conifer frame enhances outdoor pictures.

The first step is to remove the rough bark from the pole with a sharp pocketknife. Shave it off in strips, leaving the cambian layer underneath. Do not scrape down to the white wood. If the bark tends to stick in some areas, leave it intact.

Next, with the pocketknife chip the surface of the wood to produce a mottled effect. Cut the chips about ½-inch wide and up to an inch long. It just takes a flick of the wrist to cut each chip. The chips should be cut in some sort of pattern, such as a spiral, yet should not look too regular.

After creating an attractive pattern on the surface, split the pole in half, lengthwise, with a power saw or a handsaw. Sand the raw edges smooth. Cut the four sides of the frame, mitering the corners at a 45-degree angle. These corners must be cut accurately; for the best results use a miter box and backsaw.

The easiest way to join the corners of the frame is to use glue and corrugated metal fasteners. Coat both surfaces of the miter joint with glue, then lay the frame face down and drive two fasteners into the center of the joint.

If you have a router or table saw, you can mortise a recess in the back of the frame into which the picture and glass will fit. Otherwise, glue and nail thin lath, ½-inch narrower than the frame, to the back of the frame and create a recess to insert the picture and glass.

Finally, apply several coats of clear varnish to the frame. Some varnish turns yellowish with age, and if a darker tone is desired, this type should be used.

Rustic Plaques

Beautiful rustic plaques for mounting trophy heads, fish, mottos, or souvenirs can be made from a thick log. Select a log that is slightly green and do not remove the bark. To make a round plaque, saw a straight slice about 1 inch thick from the end of the log. To make an elliptical plaque, saw the slice on a diagonal. Allow the slices to dry in the shade to prevent splitting and shedding of the bark. When dry, plane and sandpaper the face and apply a few coats of varnish or lacquer.

Camera Harness

Most cameras are hard to carry. Either they swing clumsily from a strap around the neck, or they pull on

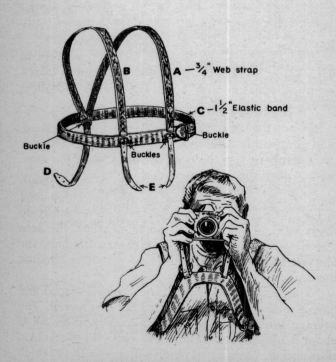

Harness holds camera snugly against chest; elastic band permits raising it quickly to the eye.

the pants in a case at the belt. To make the chore easier, I designed a harness for carrying a small camera close to the chest, without dangling, where it is always ready for taking a quick picture.

As the drawing shows, two ¾-inch web shoulder straps (A and B) are sewn to a 1½-inch elastic band (C) which buckles around the torso. At the rear of band C is sewn a ½-inch leather strap (D) with a buckle. Two other ½-inch straps (E), with buckles, are sewn to the front of the harness just below the shoulder straps. These thread through the rings on the camera and buckle it tightly against the chest. The rear strap (D) loops under the belt and is buckled.

The harness keeps the camera held securely in place, ready for instant use. When you want to take a picture, the elastic body band will stretch and allow the camera to be raised to the eye.

Combination Filter-Sunshade

If all outdoor photos could be made while shooting with the sun at one's back, there would be no need to use a sunshade. However, it is often necessary to shoot into the sun, and if sunlight strikes the lens directly, or bounces off the camera into the lens, the film can be ruined. This can be prevented by shading the lens.

Standard sunshades are usually funnel-shaped and have a metal ring which fits over the lens mount. The average sunshade for a lens of 4-inch focal length is about 3 inches long—a little too bulky to carry in a shirt pocket. Years ago, I made a filter sunshade which fits easily into a shirt pocket, and have used it consistently with a particular camera.

To make such a sunshade, get a yellow filter mounted in a metal ring that fits on your camera's lens mount. You'll also need a length of cardboard mailing tube. The inside diameter of the tube should be slightly smaller than the diameter of the filter ring. Cut a 1¼-inch length of tube and smooth both ends. Thin the rear end of the tube with a pocketknife so the filter ring will fit about ½-inch into the tube. Cement the filter ring in the tube at this point. When the cement has

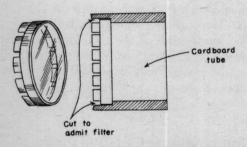

Cardboard tube

Cut to admit filter

Small filter-sunshade, made from cardboard tube, guards lens from sun's rays.

dried, paint the entire surface of the tube with flat black paint. Give the edges two coats for added protection, then wrap the tube with a couple of layers of black friction tape. The filter ring will slip on the lens mount and hold the sunshade in place.

When carrying the filter-sunshade in the shirt pocket, the glass often collects moisture and must be dried before use. To prevent this, keep the gadget in a small plastic bag. Then, when you have to take a quick picture, the filter will be dry.

Portable Background for Flower Photos

When photographing wild flowers in the woods, it is often difficult to eliminate distracting background material. You can tramp on obstructing foilage, and open wide the diaphram of the lens to blur the background, but a better method is to create an entirely new background.

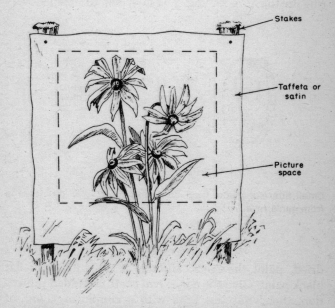

Squares of taffeta or satin in a variety of colors can be used as background for photographing wild flowers.

A few pieces of taffeta or satin, about a yard square, rolled on a cardboard tube and carried in your car, will provide you with a handy backdrop for photographing wild flowers. I have found the most useful colors to be red, blue, black, and silver. To support the backdrop, drive two sharpened stakes into the ground about a yard apart behind the flowers. Fasten the cloth to the stakes with thumbtacks.

PART 7

Horses and Horse Gear

Choosing a Suitable Horse

On most western packtrips the outfitter normally assigns each rider a horse on the basis of his experience, age, and size. A youngster usually gets a small, gentle horse; a heavy person a large, stout horse; an experienced rider a spirited horse. Occasionally, you will be given the chance to choose your own mount from those in the corral, and you should know a few things about horses to make an intelligent choice.

There is no foolproof way to choose a good horse just by looking it over. Horse buyers and professional horsemen are often fooled, giving rise to the numerous droll stories about horse swapping. Nevertheless, it is possible to observe a group of horses and eliminate the undesirables.

One basis for selecting a horse is the way it moves about the corral with other horses. If an animal constantly bites and kicks the others viciously, it is not apt to be even-tempered on the trail.

Another feature to look for is the stride of an animal. The stride should be clean; the feet should come forward in a straight line, not swing out to each side. The head should be held high, the ears and eyes should look alert. The legs should be clean and slim. Riding horses are unlike workhorses in that they don't have a lot of shaggy hair around the fetlocks.

The size of a horse is important when it is being chosen for riding on mountain trails. A slim, racy-looking animal may be fine for flat-country riding, but for mountain use a horse should have a broad chest, a strong back, and a chunky build. Reject a horse with a deeply swayed back and a pot belly.

If you are not an experienced rider, you'll want a horse that is well broken to the saddle. It's possible to single out a well-broken horse by the numerous small white patches, about the size of a thumbnail, just behind the withers and behind the shoulders in the middle of the rib cage. These marks are made by a saddle which is too tight and puts undue pressure on the horse at these points. If the horse's mane is worn just ahead of the shoulders, it may mean that it has been wearing a collar and has been used as a workhorse—that is, it is "double broken."

To gauge a horse's disposition, approach the animal and try to pet it. (Always approach a horse from the front or side, never from the rear.) If the horse lowers its ears, rolls its eyes showing the whites, and snorts, it may be too wild for anyone but an experienced rider. If the horse sidles gently away from your grasp, it is probably friendly but doesn't want to be saddled and ridden at the moment; but if it submits to a few pats on the neck and some soft words, it may be gentle enough to ride.

Once you've made your choice, and the horse has been saddled and bridled, you can put it through a final test to determine whether or not to take it on the trail. If the horse responds well to neck reining and to knee pressure, it's a good sign that it has been well trained. A horse that responds sluggishly may be slow on the trail and will have to be continually urged along the way.

How to Catch a Horse in the Open

The standard way to catch horses grazing in a meadow is first to drive them into a corral, then catch each animal by approaching it slowly and placing a halter on its head. One horse is often corraled at night and in the morning used as a wrangling horse for rounding up the others.

In areas where there is no corral, horses can be driven into a small grove of trees and confined while one or two are caught. The remaining animals often collect around those already tied. A makeshift corral of lariats tied to trees will keep horses confined while they are caught and saddled. When catching grazing horses, one should move slowly and talk gently. Yelling at a horse is the surest way to make it bolt.

A nosebag filled with a quart of grain is a good lure to use in catching a horse. Hard-working horses on a ranch are normally fed twice a day, and they quickly learn to associate the sight of a nosebag with food. Dangling a nosebag before a reluctant horse, and shaking the bag so it can hear the grain, is a good way to coax it into a halter. Soft words help, too. Once the horse can be induced to put its nose in the bag, it is an easy matter to grasp its hackamore or halter. If it's not wearing either, grasp the mane and gently drop a rope

Nosebag filled with a quart of grain is a good lure.

around its neck. The horse will generally remain still long enough to allow you to knot the rope into a loop or put on a hackamore or halter.

Halters and Bridles

The basic difference between a halter and a hack-amore is that the former is made of heavy strap leather with buckles and rings, and the latter is made of rope.

In placing a halter on a horse's head, hold the head loop in the right hand and hold the noseband open with the left. Bring the head loop up the horse's face and over the ears in one gentle movement, encircling the nose with the noseband. Free the ears from the headband and allow them to point forward in their normal position. Many horses, especially those that have been misused, dislike having their ears touched, so adjust the ears quickly and gently. Finally, bring the lower strap, or throat latch, under the throat and fasten it at the left side of the face. The horse can then be led away to be saddled, fed, or tied.

In tying a horse to a hitching rack or corral, the knot should be at about the same height as the nose, with 3 or 4 feet of slack between. A good knot is a slip knot around the pole, finished off with a half-hitch to prevent the horse from rubbing or pulling the knot undone.

The horse is controlled by a head harness called the bridle. Bridles vary in design, but they all work on the same principle. They are made of strap leather, braided leather, or rawhide. A leather band runs from the mouth area over the head and behind the ears. The two ends of the band are attached to the bit. In most models another band encircles the nose, and in some another narrow band, the throat latch, fastens under the throat.

The bit is the part of the bridle which is used to control the animal. The mouthpiece of the bit varies

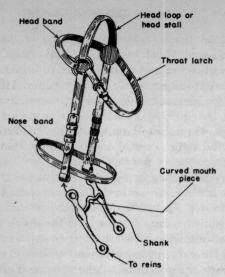

Typical horse bridle and standard bit.

according to how "hardmouthed" a horse is. A snaffle bit has a mouthpiece which is either a straight metal bar, or a bar joined at the center by two connecting loops. This type of bit is normally used for draft horses or racers. The standard bit, which is generally used when hunting on horseback or trail riding, has a mouthpiece with a mild bend at the center and long shanks. The lower ends of the shanks have loops for admitting the reins. When the reins are pulled, the curved mouthpiece presses against the roof of the horse's mouth. This pressure, and the pressure of the chin strap, causes the animal to slow or stop.

Well-trained horses are often ridden with a bridle without a mouthpiece. The horse is controlled by a snug-fitting noseband and chin strap. When the reins are tightened, the prying action of the long bit shanks restrains the horse. This bit is called a hackamore bit.

Many outfitters and guides prefer to bridle a horse over the halter or hackamore, since the animal then can be tied more securely when the rider dismounts to stalk game. The beginner should keep his horse tied by the halter rope while putting on the bridle. A horse tends to back when being bridled, and if it is not tied it may get away.

To bridle a horse, grasp the headband in the right hand, the bit in the web of the left hand, and in one easy motion lift the headband over the horse's nose so that its right side crosses the face. As the bridle is pushed upward on the face, the mouthpiece will contact the mouth. A horse accustomed to the bridle will open its mouth when the metal touches its teeth. Otherwise, place the thumb of the left hand into the mouth, behind the teeth, and press until the horse opens its mouth. Try to bridle a horse on the first try; if you fail, the horse resists even more in subsequent tries. Once the bit is in the mouth, place the headband over the ears and fasten the throat latch, if any, snugly but not tightly. During cold weather, it is advisable to warm the mouthpiece before putting it in the horse's mouth by holding it in the palm of the hand for a few minutes.

Saddling a Horse

The stock saddle is the type most commonly used for hunting and trail riding, especially in the West. This saddle has a wide pommel, a relatively low cantle, heavy skirts, and a sturdy horn. It may have one or two cinches. Such saddles weigh anywhere from 20 to 40 pounds; 30 pounds is a good weight for the average rider.

Two dimensions are important, the "swell" and the "seat." The swell, or the front width, should be 13 or 14 inches. The length of the seat may be from 13 inches, for a woman, to 16 inches, for a heavy man. A 15-inch seat is standard and will fit the average man of medium build.

The best stirrups for everyday use have flat, leather-covered bottoms. Stirrup length has to be adjusted for the individual rider, and ought to be approximately the length of his arm.

To saddle a horse, place two blankets, or one blanket and a pad, on its back so they are even on both sides. The front part of the blankets should extend

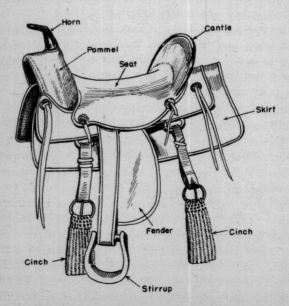

Stock saddle is used in the West for hunting and trail riding.

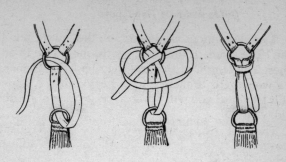

Latigo knot for fastening cinch to ring.

about 2 inches beyond the saddle skirts when the saddle is in place. If a blanket and a pad are used, the blanket goes on first. For hard riding, two blankets are necessary to protect the horse's back.

With the blankets in place, grasp the pommel and swing the saddle onto the horse, freeing the cinch or saddle strings if they catch under the saddle. Holding the horn, gently wiggle the saddle in place so that it settles snugly onto the blanket. Lift the stirrup and hook it over the horn to expose the cinch ring.

Grasp the cinch under the horse's belly, pull it up to the saddle ring, and fasten it to the ring with the latigo strap. The knot used is shown in the drawing. Some cinches are rigged with a tackberry—a metal hook that is wrapped in the latigo and hooks to the cinch ring. With a tackberry, a cinch can be tightened quicker since it is unnecessary to tie the latigo knot; the latigo is simply tightened and the knot secured.

Most horses, knowing the constriction of a tight cinch, will hold their breath while being cinched. When they exhale, the cinch will be loosened. To offset this, the cinch should be retightened before mounting.

The cinch should be checked periodically during the day. A horse sweats and loses weight, and the saddle settles after a time, causing the cinch to loosen.

If the saddle has two cinches, or is double-rigged, the rear cinch should not be as tight as the front cinch—just snug enough to touch the horse's belly. The front cinch should be tight enough so the fingers can slip between the belly and the cinch and feel a firm pressure.

When the cinch has been tightened, the stirrup is lowered and the bridle is put on.

Staking a Horse

During summer and fall, when horses are allowed to graze at night on grass in the area, it is necessary to stake them to the ground. The stake should be about 3

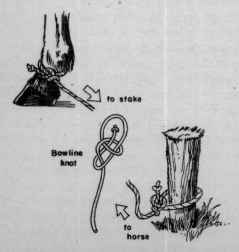

Bowline allows loops to revolve around stake as horse grazes.

feet long and 3 or 4 inches in diameter, sharpened at one end, and driven into the ground about 18 inches. A ½-inch rope from 20 to 40 feet long is used to anchor the animal to the stake. Small trees or brush within the area should be cut so they won't catch the rope as the horse feeds in a circle. Otherwise the animal may hurt itself or break loose.

It is best to tie the rope to the horse's foot rather than to its head. A horse will exert less pressure on the rope with its foot, and it is less likely to get tangled in the rope and injured. The left foot is preferred since a horse is accustomed to being handled from the left side. The best knot to use is a bowline, tied loose enough so it doesn't rub. The bowline is also used to tie the rope to the stake, as it allows the knot to revolve as the animal feeds.

A staked horse should be checked periodically, to be sure the rope hasn't tangled and to shift the stake when the animal has overgrazed its limited range.

Tethering a Horse

Sometimes a horse is tethered instead of staked—that is, it is tied by its head to a movable anchor such as a large log. This permits the horse to drag the log and prevents injury should it tangle the rope or fall. Also, the horse can feed over a wider area than if it were staked.

Horses to be tethered usually wear a halter or hackamore which has a short rope spliced to it. The tethering rope is knotted to the halter (or hackamore) rope with a bowline tied in each with the loops linked. The bowline is one of the easiest knots to untie after it has been subjected to strain.

Tethering a horse to a movable log.

An Alaskan Indian once showed me how to tether a horse on open plains where only low bushes grow. He found several little bushes growing closely together, bushes whose branches were only ½ inch in diameter. Had he tied his horse to one of them, the animal could easily have escaped. But the Indian grabbed two handfuls of bush, brought the tops together and tied them with an overhand knot. The green, flexible branches bent without breaking. He then wrapped the horse's reins tightly three turns around the knot, doubled the reins back and tied three half-hitches

Overhand
knot

Tethering a horse to low bushes.

around them. The horse was firmly tethered and could have been left for several hours if necessary.

Hobbling a Horse

In many remote areas, horse permits are issued to outfitters which allow them to graze their stock at certain prescribed spots. Most riding horses and pack stock are hobbled at night when put out to feed. If mules are used, a bell mare is hobbled among them. Mules tend to stay close to a bell mare. The outfitter may keep one horse tied at camp to help him find the hobbled stock in the 'morning.

There are many types of horse hobbles. One of the most dependable consists of two leather straps, equipped with heavy buckles, which are joined by a short chain with a swivel at the center. The straps buckle around the horse's front legs just above the fetlocks. Light hobbles, often used when a rider leaves his horse to stalk game, are made of a single strip of braided rawhide with a slit or loop at one end and a knot at the other. The leather strip is doubled and looped around one of the horse's front legs; the two ends are then twisted three or four turns and joined around the other leg.

Two types of horse hobbles: buckled straps joined by a chain and swivel; light rawhide hobble often used by hunters when stalking game.

The early Mormons invented a novel type of hobble to protect their stock from being stolen by roving bands of Indians. It consisted of rings and fastenings which had to be manipulated correctly, like a puzzle, to undo it. Before the braves could figure out how to solve the puzzle, the horse's owner would often be upon them.

Horses soon become used to hobbles, and instead of trying to take separate strides will accept the constriction and simply jump away with long bounds. Still, even an experienced hobbled horse cannot go as far in a night as can an unhobbled horse, and wranglers usually are able to locate the animal in the morning.

Feeding and Watering a Horse

If a horse is confined in a corral it usually is fed cured grain and hay three times a day. When it is to be ridden for a full day, it is fed in the morning and in the evening. An average-sized horse needs about 15 pounds, or quarter of a bale of hay, at each feeding. Alfalfa, grass, and timothy, singly or in mixture, are typical hay feeds. In addition, heavily worked horses are usually given about 2 quarts of cured grain, normally oats with a little beardless barley added. However, if a horse is fresh from the pasture and is unused to cured grain, it should be given only 1 quart or a bit more at each feeding.

When a few horses are being fed in a corral, they usually are given their hay in a manger and left untied. But if there are many horses, or if the horses are strangers to each other, it is safer to tie them at the manger by their halters or hackamores, giving them enough leeway to reach the bottom of the manger.

Grain usually is fed to horses in individual nose-bags after they have eaten their hay. All the horses should be fed grain at the same time, otherwise fights are apt to occur. Grain can be measured by cupping both hands and using them as a scoop; four handfuls make about 2 quarts.

Normally, horses require an hour or more to eat their ration of hay, about fifteen minutes to eat their nosebag of grain. Enough time should be allowed before setting out on a trip for them to eat their fill. On returning to the corral, they are fed in the same order—first hay and then grain.

Bridles should always be removed before feeding horses hay or grain. A horse can "crop" a small amount of grass along the trail while wearing a bridle, but it can't eat much dry hay with one on. If a horse is fed while tied to a tree or post, rather than at a manger, it should be checked every twenty minutes or so to see that it can reach all the hay. A feeding horse tends to nose to the bottom of a hay pile, scattering the hay beyond its reach, and the scattered hay must be swept back.

Horses in a corral should be watered after they are fed. Usually they are led by their halter ropes to a nearby stream. A horse can drink with a bridle on, but should not be compelled to except when on the trail.

When a horse is being ridden, it should never be allowed to drink its fill when overheated and sweating. It should be allowed only a few swallows, or none at all, until it cools off. Otherwise it is apt to founder.

How to Curry a Horse

A horse should be curried occasionally to remove loose hairs and dirt and to improve its appearance.

Currying also seems to improve a horse's disposition; the cleaning and grooming leave it soothed and tractable.

A steel-toothed comb and a stiff-bristled brush are used for currying. Hold the comb in the right hand, the brush in the left, and begin on the left side of the head. Brush the animal's cheeks but don't comb them unless they are unusually dirty. If combing is necessary, use a light stroke; this is a sensitive area with short hair. Always brush with the grain of the hair. Comb the forelock and mane and gently brush the forelock over the forehead and the mane toward the side it naturally lies. Then continue combing and brushing the horse's left side, working downward and back on the neck and downward over the body and legs. Exert enough pressure with the comb to remove loose hairs and dirt, but not enough to hurt the animal. Less pressure should be exerted on the brush; it is used to wipe off the loose material scraped up with the comb and to smooth the hair into a glossy coat.

Comb the tail in the same way as the mane, and then curry the right side. Give special care to the area where the saddle rides; any dirt left in this area will cause sores from the pressure of the saddle and rider.

How to Mount a Horse and Ride

When ready to mount, approach the horse from the left side, grasp the reins in the left hand, and with the same hand grasp the horse's mane just ahead of the saddle, or grasp the saddle horn. The reins should be fairly snug between the bit and the left hand. Turn the stirrup outward with the right hand, and raise the left leg and insert the toe well into the stirrup. With the right hand, grasp either the horn or the cantle of the

saddle and with a slight spring, using both arms to pull
yourself up, swing the right leg over the horse's back
and seat yourself in the saddle.

A cowboy would never turn his horse in order to
mount from the uphill side, but a beginner who has to
mount in uneven terrain should not hesitate to do so.
It's a lot easier. Only if the outfitter or owner gives you
the nod should you try to mount a horse from the right
side. Most horses won't permit it, but if a horse has
been used frequently in the mountains, it may be accustomed to being mounted from the right side, which
is often the uphill side.

The first thing to do after mounting is to straight-
en the saddle, which usually is pulled off center by the
pressure of mounting. To do this, grasp the horn and,
standing on the right stirrup, jerk the saddle to the
right.

Next, it's a good idea to check the length of the stirrups to be sure they fit properly. Even an expert horseman is unable to ride properly with stirrups of improp-
er length. If the stirrups are too long, your rump will
bump the saddle with each stride the horse takes; if too
short, you will soon develop cramps behind the knees.
Stirrups are the right length if you can stand in the
saddle, with your full weight on the stirrups, and have
1 to 2 inches of space between the saddle and your
crotch.

After adjusting the stirrups, settle into the saddle
and "find your seat." This is difficult to explain, but it is
a matter of finding the position that is comfortable both
for you and the horse. Sit straight in the saddle, not far
enough back to ride on the cantle nor far enough forward to press against the pommel. Do not twist to either side, as this will injure a horse's back. The soles of
the boots should contact the bottom of the stirrups

with a firm pressure, the heels pointing downward, and the legs should firmly grip the horse's sides.

A horse is controlled largely by the bridle reins. The reins are not used to *pull* the horse's head to one side or the other. Riding horses are trained to respond to neck-reining. To neck-rein a horse, hold the reins together in the left hand, slightly above the saddle horn, without any slack. To turn the horse to the right, move the hand holding the reins laterally to the right so the left rein lies snugly on the horse's neck. Exerting pressure on the left rein will cause the animal to turn its head to the right. At the same time, lean toward the right and press the left knee against the horse's side. These combined movements will cause a trained horse to turn to the right. To turn a horse to the left, follow the same procedure on the other side.

To start a horse from a standing position, make an exaggerated kissing sound by pursing the lips and sucking in the breath, simultaneously pressing the knees against the horse's sides. With less spirited horses, a slight kick or two with the heels is sometimes necessary.

To stop a horse, pull gently on the reins and say, "Whoa, boy!" Never pull harshly on the reins or jerk them. With a proper bit, a horse can be stopped by gentle, but firm, pressure.

It is often said that, from the outset, you should show the horse you are the boss—and it's a good maxim to follow. But it doesn't mean that you should mistreat a horse in order to dominate it. A horse should be handled with firmness and kindness. If it disobeys your wishes, correct it with a gentle voice, the proper use of the reins, and perhaps a kick or two in the ribs to accent the instructions. A horse should never be beaten, yanked by the bit, or yelled at constantly.

In mountainous country, a horse should be allowed to rest frequently. If the terrain is exceptionally steep, this may be necessary every 20 yards or so. An animal should not be permitted to climb until it lathers unduly or is exhausted. When climbing on horseback, lean forward in the saddle, and when riding downhill lean back. If the descent is steep, it's a good idea to dismount and lead the horse.

When riding across blowdown country, don't force a horse to jump over large logs. And in boggy or swampy areas, if a horse hesitates and resists crossing, trust its instinct and don't force it. Likewise, when riding along a mountain trail with numerous switchbacks, it's best to slow the horse and give it its head; the animal can normally cross bad spots on its own. The safest way of negotiating any rough terrain is to dismount and lead the horse; the difference in weight makes it easier for it to maneuver.

On crossing a stream, a horse usually wants to stop and drink, and should be allowed to. When you stop for lunch, let the horse crop grass, making sure it is safely tethered, and loosen the cinch to allow it to feed more easily.

If the ride has been long and arduous, and the animal is obviously tired, get off and walk the last mile or so into camp. Once at camp, the horse should be immediately unsaddled, fed, and watered—and left with a few kind words and a pat on the neck. This is a good horse's reward for working hard, and it expects it and deserves it.

A word about carrying extra gear on a saddle horse. If a rifle is carried in a scabbard, try to balance the weight and keep the saddle straight by carrying something on the opposite side. A compensating pressure on the stirrup on the opposite side is often sufficient to balance the saddle. Small items should be carried in a pair of small saddlebags tied behind the cantle. No more than 8 pounds should be packed in saddlebags, and the two bags should be equal in weight so they balance.

How Indians Rode

Before the Spaniards came, there were no horses in the New World. Indians in the Southwest and on the Great Plains hunted on foot and used dogs to pull their belongings. The Spaniards tried to keep horses from the Indians, but in 1680 the Pueblo Indians of New Mexico revolted and stole large herds. Thereafter,

Indian "bridle" was often a length of rawhide tied to the horse's lower jaw and used as a single rein.

horses spread across the West and changed the Indians' way of life.

Though lacking the white man's riding gear, the Indian was nevertheless a superb horseman. His saddle was usually a skin or blanket tossed over his pony's back, or lashed under the animal's belly with a length of rawhide. His bridle and reins were a length of rawhide or braided thongs tied into the horse's mouth. One method was to tie both ends of the rawhide around the horse's lower jaw and loop the rest around its neck. Another was to tie one end of rawhide around the jaw and use a single rein. The animals were trained to neck-rein.

To mount his pony, the Indian grasped its mane with both hands and pulled himself upward, balancing himself on his chest across the horse's withers. From this position, he swung his leg across the horse's back and sat upright. Or he might simply grasp a lock of mane with both hands, standing at the horse's shoulder and facing its rear, and swing himself into the saddle in one graceful motion.

How to Choose Riding Boots

The best boots for riding a horse are cowboy boots. These boots are designed especially for riding, and they are not only comfortable but have several safety features. The pointed toe slips quickly and easily into and out of the stirrup; the plain stitching of the toe sheds rain or snow; and the high arch and heel prevent the foot from slipping through the stirrup and the rider being dragged by the horse. If a boot does stick in the stirrup, it will pull off the rider's foot, leaving him free. With unpredictable horses, and in field emergencies, such features are often lifesavers.

Despite all this, the average outdoorsman has no business riding with cowboy boots unless he is accustomed to them. When using a horse for big-game hunting or camping, the majority of time is spent walking or climbing. Unless one is used to wearing cowboy boots, walking for any amount of time will cripple the feet, throw the normal posture out of line, and cause aches and undue weariness.

The best riding boot for the average outdoorsman is the one he uses for his regular outdoor activities. If one is hunting big game, the riding boot to use is the one normally worn for stalking. If one is camping, the best boot for riding is the strong, rugged shoe or boot meant for general camping.

The best all-round boot for dry-weather hunting, camping, hiking, or other summer activity is a lightweight leather boot with 6- to 8-inch uppers, "cord" soles, and leather laces. This all-purpose boot is the best choice for riding. If possible, the toes should be smooth on top, without stitching. This will help shed rain or wet snow that otherwise would collect in the seams and sink into the boot.

For very wet weather, experienced horsemen simply put a pair of rubbers arctics over their cowboy boots—the high-heeled, pointed-toe type which are especially designed for this purpose. The average outdoorsman, however, is better off in wet weather with rubber-bottomed pacs. These do not fit exceptionally well into stirrups, but since they will be used more for walking than for riding, they are the best compromise. While riding in rain or wet snow, water continuously drips on the shoes, draining down the lower legs and onto the boots. Good rubber-bottomed pacs will keep the feet dry. In cold weather, a pair of sheepskin innersoles should be used in conjunction with the pacs, to keep the feet warm while riding.

The one safety precaution to observe when riding with rubber pacs is always to keep the balls of the feet on the stirrups. In this position, the feet can easily be pulled free.

How to Shoe a Horse

Shoeing a horse correctly requires farrier's tools: a hoof knife, rasp, shoeing hammer, and pinchers. It also requires experience—and considerable strength if the horse is unwilling. Shoeing a horse string is such specialized work that many outfitters hire a professional horseshoer to do the chore for them. A good job of horseshoeing will last approximately a month on stock which is daily traversing rocky mountain country. Often the shoes will last a full hunting season, but if a shoe does pull off, and you are without professional help, it is useful to know how to replace it. This can be done with nothing more than a horse rasp, horseshoe nails, and a claw hammer. An average riding horse takes a #2 shoe and #5 and #6 horseshoe nails.

Tie the horse with a short rope to a tree or hitching rack on level ground. Place the tools near the foot to be shod, so that, once started, you can do the job as rapidly as possible. A horse dislikes having its foot held up for a long time.

To shoe a horse's front foot, stand at the animal's shoulder and grasp the hairs of the foot at the pastern joint. Pull the front foot upward, and say, "Raise up." A horse previously shod will usually raise its foot at this command. If not, pulling up on the hairs will cause the horse to raise its foot.

When the foot is raised, place it between your knees, facing the horse's rear, and hold it there firmly. Using the rasp, clean the frog of the hoof of any gravel

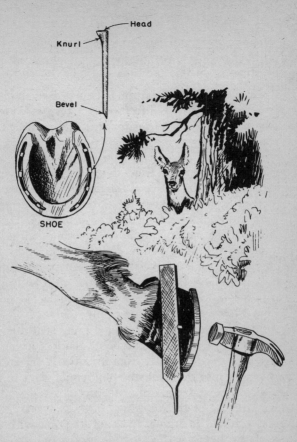

Horseshoe nails are driven through slot and into hoof at a slight angle so they will protrude from the side. Points are then twisted off with claw hammer, clinched and filed smooth.

or rocks, and then smooth down the entire bottom surface. It the animal has been previously shod and has just slipped a shoe, the surface of the hoof need only be smoothed down for about ⅛ to ¼ inch. Next, smooth the edges by rubbing them with the rasp at right angles.

Now place the shoe on the flat surface of the hoof to see whether it fits. If the shoe is a bit too wide, it must be heated (even in a campfire) and then held at the center with a pair of tongs or pliers, and the ends pounded slightly together. If too narrow, the heated shoe must be spread a trifle by pounding it over a pointed rock that fits between the points of the shoe.

Once the shoe has been fitted, hold it in place and nail it to the hoof with four nails on each side. This is the vital part of the operation. A horseshoe nail is not symmetrical; the head bends slightly to one side and the point of the nail is beveled. In placing the nail into the slot of the shoe, the head of the nail *must* be tipped towards the inside of the hoof and the beveled point must head towards the outside of the hoof.

In driving the nail, the beveled point will then go approximately ¾ inch into the hoof, gently curving so that it will protrude slightly from the side. If driven the opposite way into the hoof, the nail would slant in the other direction and penetrate deeply into the central part, or "quick," of the hoof.

As each nail is driven, twist off its point with the claws of the hammer. To do this, grasp the nail between the claws and twist clockwise. The nail will break at the junction with the hoof. Twisting off the point is necessary, for if a horse lowers its leg while the nail protrudes, it may sink into your leg. This is why professional horseshoers wear a leather apron.

When all eight nails are driven, and twisted off, the hoof may be lowered temporarily so the horse can rest. While it rests, smooth the part of the hoof just below each protruding nail. The hoof will be broken at these points and must be smoothed so the nails can be clinched. Use a corner of the rasp to do this.

Again lift the hoof, hold it between your legs, and place the edge of the rasp at the point where each nail protrudes from the hoof. Tap the head with the hammer. If the rasp is held flat against the hoof, the broken ends of the nails will be bent outwards. After each end has been tapped against the rasp, finish the clinching with the hammer, tapping the ends against the hoof and giving each a light stroke with the rasp.

The average person should not attempt to shoe the hind feet until he has had considerable experience in shoeing the front feet. It's harder for a horse to stand with its hind foot lifted, and many horses will kick anyone trying to fit a shoe on the hind foot. It is more important to be able to replace a front shoe than a rear one, since a horse can travel without a rear shoe more easily than it can without a front shoe.

Tying a String of Horses

When several packhorses are taken on a trip, they are often tied together to prevent them from feeding along the trail or running off. But it is necessary to fasten them together so that if one horse stumbles and falls over a bluff, it won't pull the entire string with it. Western outfitters generally use a length of rope spliced into a circle, one end of which goes over the tree of the packsaddle of the first horse and is connected with baling twine to the halter or hackamore rope of the horse behind it. Another spliced loop ties in the next horse in the string, and so on down the line. The sisal twine is strong enough to hold the horses on the trail, but will break if one falls.

If a wrangler has to bring in several unsaddled horses over smooth terrain, he often uses a different method—called "tailing" the stock. The tail of the first animal in the string is folded into a loop, just below the fleshy part, and is attached to the halter or hackamore rope of the horse behind it with a special knot, as shown in the drawing. The other horses are joined in the same way, one behind the other.

But even tailing can be hazardous. In Wyoming, two hunters decided to bring in a fresh bearskin on a horse unused to the smell of bear. After several unsuccessful attempts to load the hide, they had to blindfold the horse and tail it up short to a gentle horse named

Special knot used for tailing horses on smooth terrain.

Brownie. When they removed the blindfold, the loaded horse went berserk. As one of the hunters described it, "He reared and bucked like fresh out of a buckin' chute. He jerked so hard Brownie was lifted clean off his hind feet—his rear end never did come down for thirty minutes!"

How to Make a Rope Hackamore

If a standard hackamore is not available, a horse is often led by a rope tied around its neck. This isn't always satisfactory, for an animal so tied is hard to handle and tends to pull back or graze unduly. There are two ways, however, to make a hackamore out of a rope tied by a bowline around a horse's neck. As shown in the drawings, the hackamore knot forms a nose loop which aids in controlling a horse.

The simplest way to tie a hackamore knot is to grasp the rope near the bowline and double it into a loop about 20 inches long. Tie two overhand knots in the loop, and snug the finished knot close to the bowline. This loop forms the noseband. Then undo the bowline around the horse's neck, slip the loop over its nose, and retie the bowline to fit.

The second hackamore knot is a little more complicated, but it's a favorite of veteran horsemen and worth knowing. To learn to tie this knot, get a few feet of rope and practice without a horse. Hold the rope with both hands palm upward, one end extending about 18 inches from the right hand. Now, gripping the rope with the fingers, turn the palms down. You'll find that you've formed two loops. Lay the loops on a table so they form a figure like the one in the drawing. The strands in the drawing are numbered 1, 2, 3, and 4. Following the path of the arrow, reach over strand

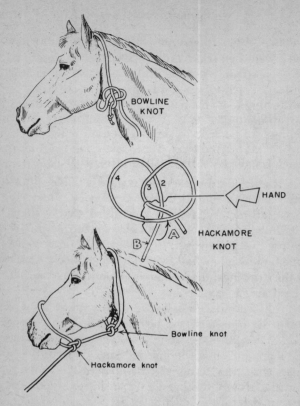

BOWLINE KNOT

HAND

HACKAMORE KNOT

Bowline knot

Hackamore knot

Hackmore knot forms a nose loop which helps in controlling a horse.

number 1, under 2, over 3, under 4, and around the running end, B, and grasp the rope at point A. Holding both ends in the left hand, pull with the right hand— and you've tied the hackamore knot.

Once you've mastered forming the loops and reaching through to tie the knot, try tying the hackamore on a horse. Use the animal's neck to support the loops, and once the nose loop has been formed, retie the bowline to take up any slack.

How to Whip a Rope End

The simplest way to keep a sisal rope from unraveling is to tie an overhand knot at each end. But when a rope has to be threaded through small rings an overhand knot won't work. The solution is to whip the end with a strong cord. Silk casting line is good for whipping, but any strong cord is suitable.

To whip a rope, lay one end of the cord along the rope so it protrudes a few inches from the end, as shown in Figure 1 of the drawing. Starting about 1½

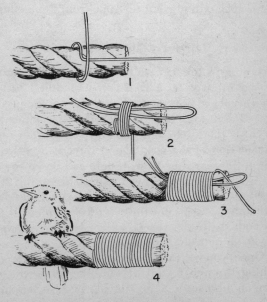

Steps in whipping a rope end.

inches from the end (for a rope of ⅝ inch diameter),
wind the cord around the rope and over its own end.
Draw each wrapping tightly against the previous one.
After two or three turns, cut a 6-inch piece of the
whipping cord, double it, and hold it over the wrapping as you continue to wind (Figure 2). When you
have wrapped ¼ inch from the end, thread the end of
the whipping cord through the loop (Figure 3), and
pull the two protruding ends of the loop. This will bury
the end under the wrapping (Figure 4). Snip off the
end, and the whipping is completed.

The end of a nylon rope can be finished more easily. Merely pass a lighted match once or twice under it.
The quick heat of the match will melt the fibers without burning the rope, and the result is a small glazed
"knot" which will prevent the rope from unraveling.

How to Throw a Sling Hitch

A sling hitch generally is used to lash cargoes
wrapped in tarps on a Decker packsaddle. With this
hitch, cargoes of uneven weight or size can be perfectly
balanced and don't have to be packed in panniers.

To tie the hitch, knot the end of the sling rope to
the front ring of the saddle, and thread the other end
through the rear ring, as in Figure 1. Loosen the cross
loop sufficiently so the cargo will fit inside it. Lift the
cargo high on the side of the saddle, and holding it
there with one arm, put the cross loop around it. Then
grasp the vertical rope, pull it under the cargo, and
draw it tight. Bring the rope up the side of the cargo, over the cross rope, and push a small loop (A in
Figure 2) under the strand. Pull down on A, tightening
the hitch. Grasping the rope at B in Figure 2, pull it
through loop A. The resulting knot is shown untight-

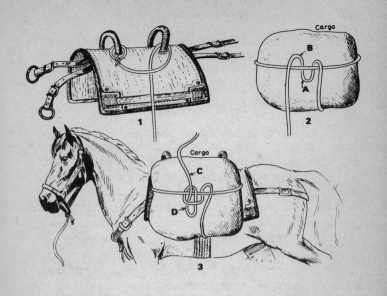

Sling hitch tied on a Decker packsaddle.

ened, for clarity, in Figure 3. To complete the hitch, grasp the rope at C and tie two half hitches around loop D.

The other cargo is lashed to the right side of the horse in the same way, but the sling rope is knotted to the rear ring. When both cargoes have been loaded and hitched, they are further secured by running the remaining rope of one hitch across the top of the saddle, pushing it through loop D and bringing it back over the saddle again.

Loads of uneven weight are balanced as they are hitched. The heavier one should be held high on the saddle and tied there with the cross rope, the lighter one allowed to ride farther down, over the curve of the horse's body. This balances the uneven weight.

How to Throw a Barrel Hitch

The barrel hitch is often used with a Decker or a sawbuck packsaddle for packing elongated cargoes such as the hind quarters of elk or package of tents and poles. The drawings show how it is tied on a sawbuck saddle.

First, tie the end of the lash rope securely to the front sawbuck, as shown in Figure 1. Form a loop below the front sawbuck, bring the running end back over the front sawbuck and over and behind the rear sawbuck, forming a second loop. The end of the rope should now be hanging from the rear sawbuck.

Insert the cargo in the loops (Figure 2). Tighten the front loop so that the cargo is in the correct position, and take up the slack toward the rear loop. Tighten the rear loop, bring the running end under the cargo and up to rope A, and tie it with two half-hitches.

Lash the second cargo to the other side of the pack animal in the same manner. Elk quarter should be covered with tarps, but they may be packed as shown if none is available.

How to Throw a Diamond Hitch

The diamond hitch is the best-known hitch for lashing down a load on a packhorse or mule. It is normally used after the cargoes have been lashed on with another type of hitch or the panniers have been loaded, and a top pack, covered with a canvas tarp, has been

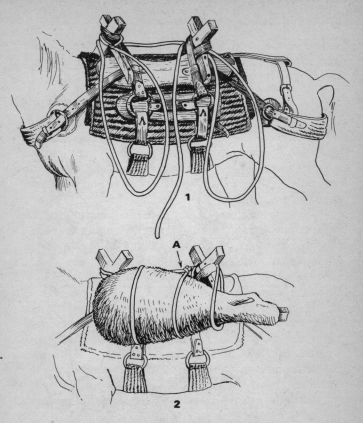

Barrel hitch tied on a sawbuck packsaddle.

added. The diamond hitch is used with both sawbuck and Decker packsaddles.

A lash rope about 25 feet long is needed to throw a diamond hitch. One end is knotted (called the running end); the other end is tied to a cinch.

Stand at the horse's left shoulder and lay the run-

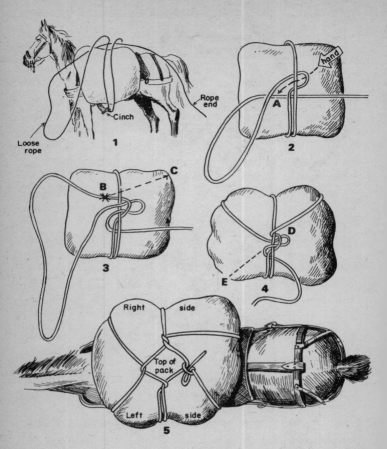

Diamond hitch.

ning end of the rope along the top of the load so it extends to the horse's tail. Wrap the cinch end of the rope around the horse and load, and catch the rope in the cinch hook (Figure 1). Allow the loose rope to fall to the ground at the horse's shoulder.

Bring the loose rope over the strand that runs along the length of the horse and tuck a small loop under the strand that encircles the horse and pack (Figure 2). Reach under this loop, over the encircling strand, and grasp point A. Pull the rope through the loop, forming a second loop (Figure 3). Grasp the rope at point B (Figure 3), tighten the hitch, and pull this rope across to point C (Figure 4) and under the pack. Now grasp the rope at point D (Figure 4) and bring it under the top pack at point E. Tie the end of the rope, as shown in Figure 5, with a looped half-hitch. When seen from the top, the center of the hitch will form a diamond.

The beauty of the diamond hitch is that no segment of the rope is tied but is free to distribute the tension of the hitch over the entire rope. In effect, this prevents any section of the hitch from loosening.

How to Throw a McNeel Hitch

The McNeel hitch often is used instead of the diamond hitch to lash down cargoes or panniers after they have been secured to the packsaddle with a sling hitch.

To throw the hitch, stand at the left side of the horse and toss the cinch end of the lash rope across the animal's back, over the load. Grasp the cinch as it comes under the horse and hook the lash rope on the left side of the animal, under the load at the belly line. Two turns with the rope are made in the cinch hook, as shown in Figure 1.

Maintaining tension on the rope at the cinch hook, form a large half-hitch in the running end, large enough to completely encircle the cargo (Figure 1). The end of

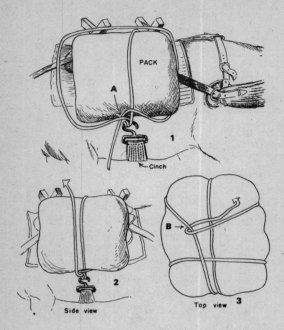

McNeel hitch.

the rope should come *under* the half-hitch just above
the cinch hook (A).

Tighten the half-hitch around the left-side cargo
by pulling the running end, as shown in Figure 2, and
bring the rope to the top of the load.

At this point, bring the running end across the
saddle to the forward end of the right-side cargo, down
the front end, under, and up the rear end. The lash
should look like Figure 3, which is a top view. Run the
end under the lash at point B. Tighten the rope and
tie at B with a looped half-hitch, completing the job.

How to Throw a Gilligan Hitch

Professional outfitters and packers display a fierce pride toward their work. No professional packer will admit that any horse or mule is too tough for him to handle. Once in the hills with his packstring, a packer will never give up on an unruly animal. A packer friend, on one occasion where a mule lay down, told me quietly, "I'll load that mule or kill him." He loaded the mule. A packer is also proud of the appearance of his loaded packstring. He simply will not be caught in the company of another packer with his cargoes looking sloppy. After a long pack on a tough mountain trail, he will stop his string within a quarter-mile of base camp and repack his cargoes so that his outfit will look shipshape when he arrives.

In the Selway country years ago, there was a packer named Gilligan, who reputedly came into camp one day with his packs in a mess. Tarps were dragging, half off the mules; cargoes were tipped to one side; and blankets had slipped halfway out behind the saddles. Being very tired, Gilligan hadn't made that final stop to reshape his load.

And so to this day a sloppy job of packing is known as a Gilligan hitch.

Therefore, the way to throw a Gilligan hitch is simply to take a length of rope, some duffel, and a pack animal, and begin tying things on without rhyme or reason.

How to Make Shotgun Chaps

A pair of chaps is indispensable to anyone who rides a great deal in heavily wooded terrain where branches and brush tear cloth pants to shreds. The best type for dry-weather riding is a pair of shotgun chaps, which take their name from the slimness of the legs. These chaps may be obtained at a riding outfitter, but if you have a tanned deerskin or elk skin you may want to make your own, largely for the fun of doing it and for the pleasure of wearing clothing of your own making.

You'll need a pattern from which to cut the chaps from the skin. If you already own a pair of store-bought chaps, you can of course use them as a model for cutting a paper pattern. Otherwise, an old pair of work pants will serve as a pattern. Put them on and have someone mark them for cutting as shown in the drawing.

The first mark begins at the top of the outside seam, at the belt line, and angles across one buttock, under the crotch, and up one side of the fly to the front belt line. The other leg is marked in the same way. Another mark runs down the outside of each leg, beginning 1 inch from the first mark at the top of the outside seam, and goes straight down the leg to the cuff, ending 2 inches behind the seam. The marks that end at the top of the fly are then rounded off to form the characteristic "belt" of the chaps. This mark should begin 3 inches below the belt line and curve across the front to a point 3 inches from the original mark.

After the pants have been marked correctly, cut out the pattern with a pair of scissors. This pattern is not necessarily the true pattern, since the pants from which it was cut may have been a little too large or too small. The standard sizes for the legs of shotguns chaps are as follows: for slim builds—22 inches wide at the top of the thigh; for medium

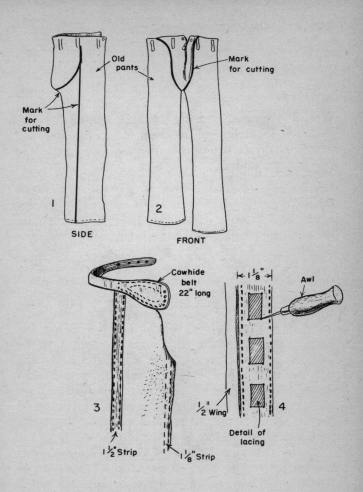

1 SIDE

Old pants

Mark for cutting

2 FRONT

Mark for cutting

Cowhide belt 22" long

3

1½" Strip

1⅛" Strip

1⅛"

½" Wing

4

Awl

Detail of lacing

Mark pattern for chaps (Figures 1 and 2) on pair of old pants. Figure 3 shows position of strips and belt, with detail of lacing in Figure 4.

builds—23 inches; for heavy builds—24 inches. The legs taper to 20 inches at the bottom.

Lay the pattern on the skin and adjust the measurement to suit your particular physique. This adjustment, if necessary, is made on the inside of the legs. Then add 1½ inches for the seam. When the measurements are correct, mark the leather and cut out the legs with a sharp knife.

Buckskin lacing

Finished chaps laced in front with buckskin.

The next step is to make the belt for the chaps. This should be cut from medium-heavy cowhide. It consists of two pieces. Each piece conforms to the curved top of the legs. It should taper from 3 inches at the front to 1½ inches around the side and back. One piece is fitted with a buckle at the small end, the other terminates in a pointed strap with holes. Each belt half should be about 22 inches long, allowing for riveting the buckle and for wearing the chaps over the pants.

Sew the belt halves to the legs, or give the material to a shoemaker and let him do it on a machine.

It is now necessary to reinforce the edges of the legs, and this too is a good job for a shoemaker. Cut two strips of leather the same length as the legs, one 1⅛ inches wide, the other 1½ inches wide. Sew the 1⅛ inch strip to the front-outside edge, leaving a small wing of the leg material as shown. Sew the 1½ inch strip on the inside of the rear edge of the leg material, flush with the edge (that part coming from the rear and which will be underneath). As shown in the drawing, the strips are sewn with two seams.

The edges of each leg can now be laced together to form the "barrels" of the shotgun. To do this, cut a lace of ½-inch leather somewhat longer than the legs. Using an awl, punch a series of holes through the outside strip and the leg, as shown in the drawing, and cut the leather between each set to make a slit. Now turn this strip down on the inside strip and use the first set of holes as a template to punch the second set, thereby making sure all the holes line up. When holes have been punched in both legs, lace the edges of each leg together, and rivet the ends of each lace to keep it from pulling out. While you're riveting, it's a good idea to rivet the belt at the point where it leaves the leg. This will prevent the stitches from tearing.

The legs of the chaps must now be fastened at the front of the belt. This is done by punching a matched set of holes in the front ends of the belt and lacing them together with a length of ¼-inch buckskin. Lacing is used here instead of rivets or a buckle so that if a rider is thrown, and his belt catches on the saddle horn, it will break apart.

PART 8

Miscellaneous How-To

Loseproof Pocketknife Case

If you have a habit of losing your pocketknife in the outdoors when you most need it, here's a simple case you can make from a strip of thin leather that will fit in your pocket and secure the knife to your belt.

For an average-sized pocketknife you'll need a strip of leather about 20 inches long and 1½ inches wide. Cut it according to the pattern shown in the drawing. Fold the 1½-inch width back on itself and sew together the three edges. Then turn the case thus formed inside-out.

Cut a ½-inch slit in the case ⅜ inch from the top (see drawing). Cut another slit 1 inch long and ½ inch from the end of the narrow strip. That's all there is to making the case.

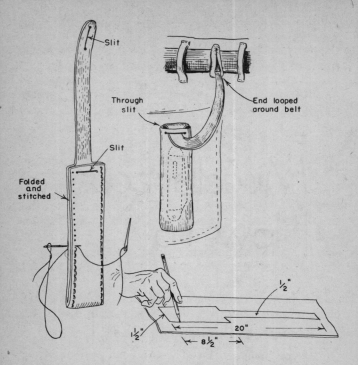

Strap keeps pocketknife case closed and secured to belt.

Insert the knife, pass the end of the strip through the slit in the case, and pull it tight, sealing in the knife. Slip the end of the strip through your belt, pass the case through the slit in the end, and drop it in your pocket. You'll never lose your pocketknife again.

Survival Knife

This is a handy tool to take along on outdoor trips. Made from a power hacksaw blade, it will cut or saw the toughest materials, yet it's small enough to tie to the frame of a packboard for use in an emergency.

Get a 16-inch blade and cut it in half on the edge of an emery wheel. Cut it at an angle, with the teeth on the long side. Then grind the blade to the shape of a skinning knife, rounding off the diagonal end, and leaving a few inches for a handle. Grind slowly, cooling the blade often, so as not to draw the temper of the steel. When the blade has been ground to the proper shape, sharpen the smooth edge on the wheel, and then hone it on a stone to a fine finish. Finally, wrap the handle with a few turns of electrician's tape, leaving the hole in the end exposed. Then tie a length of buckskin thong in the hole with which to tie the knife to a packboard or other safe place.

A standard hacksaw blade can be turned into a smaller knife in the same way. This one will be about 3 inches overall, but it will do many small cutting jobs.

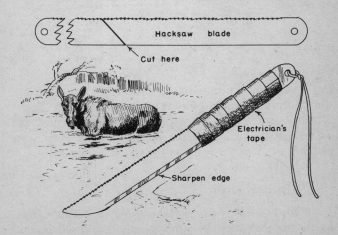

Survival knife from hacksaw blade.

How to Make Knives

Hunters with an unmounted deer, elk, or moose rack can use the antlers for making handsome knife handles. A variety of blades are available that can be transformed into rugged knives by anyone who can work with tools.

Start with a kitchen paring knife, or a larger utility knife with a 5-inch blade. The knife should be of top-quality steel, as it is foolish to expend time and energy on making a handle if the blade is inferior. A paring knife makes a good fish knife, a utility knife a good hunting knife. For the handle, select a length of tine

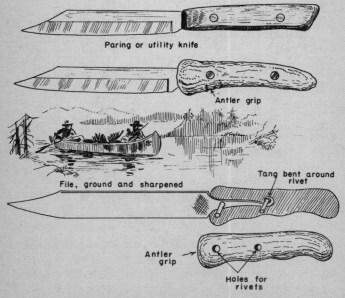

Paring or utility knife fitted with antler grip (top). Knife made from file (bottom) is secured in grip by bending tank around rivet.

from a deer antler. The wide end, where it joins the main beam, serves as a hilt, tapering to a narrow butt.

With a backsaw, saw the tine in half lengthwise. Mark the position of the holes in the blade, and carefully drill the handle from the outside. Attach the antler halves to the blade with long copper rivets, filing off the heads of the rivets and tapping them in place with a ball-pein hammer. Smooth and polish the ends of the rivets so they are nearly flush with the handle.

A more challenging job is to make your own blade from an old file. A 6-inch flat bastard file is suitable. Grind it slowly on an emery wheel into the shape of a knife blade, being sure not to draw the temper of the steel. When the blade has been shaped and nearly sharpened, bore a hole through the large part of the tang.

To attach the antler handle, it's necessary to chisel a small mortise on the inside surface of each half. This mortise should be cut to the shape of the tang, and only as deep as half its thickness. Outline the tang with a pencil on the antler surface to get the correct shape.

When the mortise has been cut, hold the tang in the mortise, mark the position of the hole, and drill through both halves of the handle. Then drill a second hole in each half about 1 inch from the butt.

Fit the antler halves on the tang and rivet them in place. If the mortise has been cut accurately, the two rivets will hold the handle firmly on the tang. However, if the fit is not exact, or if the blade is long, the tang can be secured firmly to the handle by bending its tip into a small loop, boring another hole in the handle aligned with this loop, and installing another rivet. The blade can then be honed to a fine edge.

A few companies, such as the Indian Ridge Traders of Ferndale, Michigan, sell knife blades without

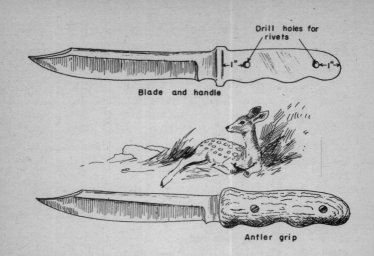

Drill holes for rivets

1"   1"

Blade and handle

Antler grip

Blade and tang handle

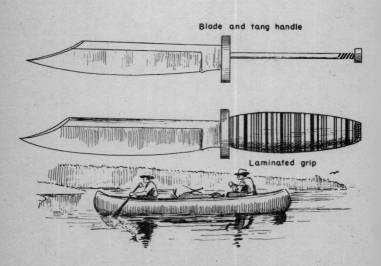

Laminated grip

Knives without grips are available for the do-it-yourselfer.

handles especially for the do-it-yourselfer. The blades come with tangs or with round rods. Those with rods can be fitted with laminated handles of leather, aluminum, hard rubber, or antler.

How to Make Rustic Furniture

Chipped conifers, which were described in the article on making picture frames, will make attractive rustic furniture for summer homes. The basic tools needed are a saw and a power drill or hand brace with extension bits up to 1¼ inches in diameter.

The table shown in the drawing is a good piece for the beginner to build. The legs are about 4 inches in diameter and 30 inches long, the rails 2 inches in diameter, their length determined by the table's size. Remove the bark and chip the legs and rails, but do not varnish them, before assembling the table.

Two sets of rails join the legs together and brace the table. The top rail is set 2 inches from the top of the legs, the second rail 6 inches. The rails can be made of saplings 2 inches in diameter.

When cutting the rails to size, allow 4 inches at each end for inserting them in holes in the legs. Taper each rail end with a pocketknife or drawknife to a diameter of 1¼ inches. The rail ends should taper sharply from the original diameter; the last 2 inches should be uniform in diameter. Tapering will remove the chipped bark, but the white wood will look attractive on the finished piece.

Bore 1¼-inch holes 2 inches deep in the top of the legs to receive the rails. As an aid in boring the holes at a true right angle, it helps to scribe a right angle, with a square, on the top of each leg. Align the bit with these marks as you drill and the holes will be true.

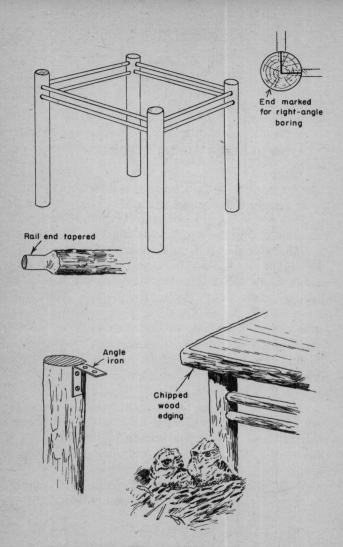

End marked
for right-angle
boring

Rail end tapered

Angle
iron

Chipped
wood
edging

Leg and rail assembly for building rustic table. Top is attached with angle irons.

Assemble the rails and legs with glue.

The top can be made of ¾-inch plywood. It should extend beyond the legs 4 inches on each side. Finish the edges by gluing on half-round branches chipped to match the legs and rails.

At this stage, sand the top, and the legs and rails where necessary, and finish with a couple of coats of varnish.

Attach the top with 4-inch angle irons. Use lag screws to attach the angle irons to the legs, flatheaded wood screws to attach the irons to the top.

A rustic bed can be made of chipped conifers using the same leg-and-rail method. Use two short posts for the footboard and two longer posts for the headboard, with two rails along the sides and ends. Cross rails support the box spring and mattress. The foot-

Rustic bed is built with same leg and rail assembly.

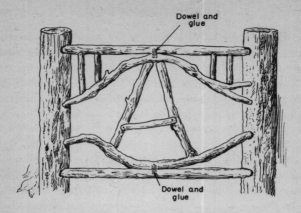

Decorative headboard displays owner's initial.

Elliptical log slab can be turned into a handsome coffee table.

board may be braced with a crossbar between the posts. The headboard is braced with a crossbar near the top.

A more elaborate headboard can be created by using curved branches, either to form a symmetrical design or your own initials.

If you can obtain an extra-large log, and can persuade a sawmill to saw off an elliptical slab about 3 inches thick, you can turn it into an attractive coffee table. The slab should be dried indoors before working on it. When it has cured without splitting or shedding its bark, sand one side smooth. Bore four holes in the underside of the slab, angling outwards, and fit four short legs of chipped-wood saplings. Glue the legs in place and shape the ends to stand flat on the floor.

Antler Door Handles and Drawer Pulls

Deer antlers make attractive door handles and drawer pulls for summer homes and other places where a rustic decor is appropriate. Generally the smaller tines on an antler are the right size for handles and pulls, and they should be slightly curved. When cutting the tine for a door handle, include part of the main beam at the joint. This is rounded off and forms the top of the handle. The ends must be ground flat so they butt evenly against the surface on which the handle or pull is mounted. Drill a hole through each end of the tine, and attach it to the wood with Phillips-head screws.

Handles, and especially pulls, can also be installed so that the screws don't show. To do this, drill holes smaller than the diameter of the Phillips-head screw on the face of each end of the antler. Measure the distance

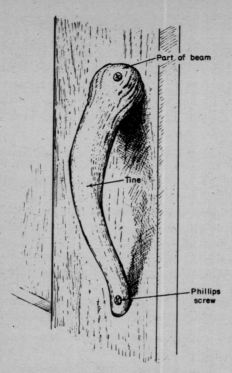

Part of beam

Tine

Phillips
screw

Door handle made from deer antler.

between the two holes and transfer the points to the wooden surface. Then drill holes in the door or drawer and attach the handle with screws from the inside.

Sagebrush Ornaments

The lowly sagebrush can be made into beautiful ornaments for decorating tables and floral arrangements. Dry wood is best for the purpose, and one way of obtaining it is to search out stands of sagebrush, cut dead bushes at their base with a sharp ax, remove the bark, and use them according to their particular forms. The living bushes also can be cut green and carefully dried in a shed. Then the light, stringy bark can be peeled off in long strips.

There are two fine ways to finish sagebrush. One is to wipe the surface free of all particles of bark and coat it with varnish or lacquer. This will impart a brownish color to the wood, varying in shade depending on the age of the brush and the thickness of the bark. Under clear varnish or lacquer, tiny pepper-like flecks will show up over the entire surface. The second way is to chip the surface with a pocketknife, as described in making picture frames and rustic furniture. Finish with a coat of shellac, or a light stain that blends with the decor of the room and a coat or two of clear varnish.

Chopping Mitts

A pair of loose-fitting leather mitts is handy to have around camp for picking up hot utensils, handling rough wood for the campfire, and especially for using an ax. In cold weather they can be worn over regular gloves. You can make a pair of mitts from the tanned skin of a moose, elk, or deer.

First trace the outline of your hand on a piece of paper, with the fingers together. Allow sufficient space around the thumb for a seam, and extend the pattern well over the wrist.

Fold the leather and place the pattern so that the outside edge of the hand aligns with the fold. The fold forms one side of the mitt, leaving only the top and the thumb side to be sewn or laced. Double stitch the mitts on a sewing machine, using a strong nylon or linen thread. If your sewing machine won't handle the weight of the leather, take the mitts to a shoemaker.

For a more attractive seam, lace the edges of the mitts with the same leather or one of contrasting color. Stagger the holes ½-inch apart to prevent the lace from drawing the edges out of shape. Begin lacing at the wrist, running the end under the first few stitches, and hiding the other end at the completion of the stitching in the same way.

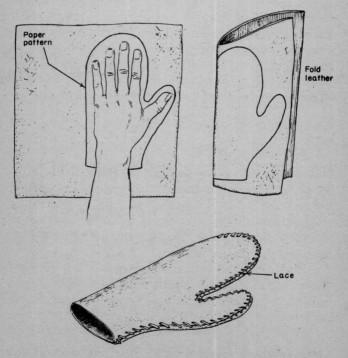

Trace paper pattern of hand on leather, fold at outside mark, and cut double thickness. Lace the open side.

Leather Vest

To make a vest from a tanned elk skin or deerskin, cut a pattern from an old shirt, using colored chalk to mark the cutting lines on the shirt while you're wearing it. With the collar unbuttoned, mark the top edge of the shoulder seam (see drawing), the seam that joins the collar to the shirt, and down the front seam to a point 3 inches above the belt. Continue the cutting line

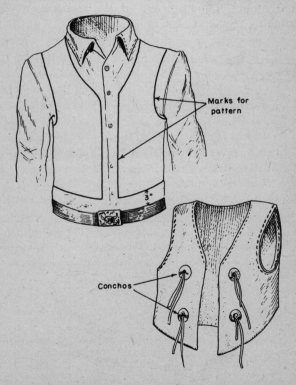

Mark pattern for vest on old shirt. Stitch arm holes and front, attach conchos.

around the body to the center of the back. Mark the other side in the same way. Cut the shirt along these lines, and then cut the side seams of the shirt, separating the front half of the pattern from the back. You now have three patterns—the back and two sides. Trace them on the unfinished side of the leather. Before cutting, extend the edges where the seams will be sewn so there's sufficient room for stitching.

The simplest method of sewing the vest is with two straight seams at each edge, so that the garment can be turned inside-out and the stitching will be on the inside. If the raw edges of the stitching irritate the shoulders, turn these edges back against the leather and stitch them flat.

An attractive way to join the shoulders is to lace the edges together, overlapping them like the sides of the shotgun chaps (which see).

If heavy leather is used, the arm holes and front edges may be left as is. For vests of buckskin or other light leather, stitch a 1-inch strip of leather on the front edges, around the neck and arm holes. Simply fold the strip of leather over the edge and sew the three thicknesses together with a single seam.

Finish the vest with decorative conchos fastened to the front, 2 inches from the edges, with a loop of leather thong threaded through horizontal slots cut in the vest.

How to Pan for Gold

One of the most exciting activities in wilderness country is to pan for gold in unexploited creek beds. The standard gold pan that is made for this purpose is the best utensil to use, but the go-light backpacker is unlikely to have one along. An ordinary steel skillet can be used for gold panning, although it's slower than the gold pan.

Before setting to work in a creek bed, burn the skillet over a fire so that its bottom is not only free of grease but has turned blue. This is important; gold particles will show up well against such a color.

Start the gold search by scooping several handfuls of gravel into the skillet, submerging the skillet in water, and gently swishing it about until the water and gravel are thoroughly mixed. Gold particles often stick to large rocks and must be washed into the skillet.

Pick out the largest rocks first and then carefully pour out the water. Dip more water into the skillet and swish it around. Pick out the smaller rocks, and repeat the process. In pouring out the water, just tip the skillet gently, allowing the water to slip over the rim. Continue until there is nothing left in the skillet except tiny grains of black sand and the smallest particles of gravel.

At this stage, fill the skillet with water, swish it around, and pour most of it out, leaving just enough to cover the bottom. Gently swish the water around the bottom, and slowly tip the skillet toward you. The gold particles will remain on the bottom while the water and sand flows away. The gold will show up as brilliant yellow against the blue skillet.

Pick out any small particles of gold in the skillet. If only gold dust shows, pour it into a small bottle together with the black sand that will be mixed with it. When the sand is dry, pour it back in the skillet and gently blow it away from the gold dust. Then pour the dust back into the bottle.

Novice prospectors usually fail to find gold dust on their first tries because they don't dig deep enough for gravel. Gold is heavier than other earth materials and sinks into the ground under the weight of flowing water. Thus gold usually is found on the bedrock of a creek rather than in the gravel on top. Gravel bars on the inside of creek bends, which have built up through the ages, are good places to pan.

Rock Hunting

This is a fascinating hobby that ties in perfectly with other outdoor activities. Here are a few hints for spotting unusual rocks and semiprecious stones as you hike.

Be on the lookout for rocks that don't blend with others in the immediate area. Often such specimens have broken off larger rocks and been moved by water to a new location. That's why dry washes in arid or semiarid country are good places to look. During spring runoff, many rocks and gems are uncovered or brought downstream by the current. In larger rivers whose water levels change drastically, such as the Yukon in Canada, the gravel bars are alternately washed and built up, and contain millions of small rocks. Specimens of agate and jasper abound. When wet by the current, these appear much as they will when polished.

Investigate egg-sized or larger rocks that are crusted with a hard coating and have many little "warts" on their surface. These may be semiprecious stones.

Petrified wood is often ash-white on the surface, nearly black inside. It is heavier than ordinary wood, and contains the annual growth rings of the original tree.

Jade, which is found in parts of Alaska and Wyoming, often looks like a green rock. The rock may be anywhere from a very light green to a dark, nearly black shade. Jade also can be identified by its soft, soapy feeling.

The best way of testing a stone to determine whether it will polish well is to wet it. If it dries with a dull luster it's probably just another rock, but if it takes on a bright finish it may be jewelry material.

A rock hammer is a valuable tool for searching and testing. The head has a pick on one side and a square, flat surface on the other. The flat head is designed for chipping off a corner of a rock so you can see the inside. (Never break a possible valuable specimen in the center.) A round-headed hammer will shatter the rock, but the square surface of the rock hammer's head chips away only a tiny sliver at a blow.

Small gems or unusual stones can be polished in a special rock-tumbling machine that costs from $15 and up. A quantity of rocks is put in the tank, an abrasive and a polisher are added, and an electric motor "tumbles" the mixture until the stones take on a high luster. The abrasive must be changed periodically. It takes approximately six weeks of tumbling to polish a group of rocks.

Large rocks must be cut to the proper shape and size if they are to be used for jewelry. This is usually done with a diamond saw. The desired contours are shaped on a grinding wheel, and the rocks are then polished in a tumbler.

Make Your Own Leather Tools

Tools for working leather can be made of ordinary spikes ranging in size from 20d to 60d. With these simple tools it is possible to create attractive designs in homemade leather articles.

Clamp the spikes in a vise and file the tops of their

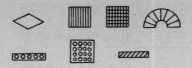

Tools you can make from nail heads for decorating leather.

heads perfectly flat. Then file the heads into various shapes. A square, crescent, diamond, fan, and bar are four usable shapes which can be combined to tool designs in leather. They may vary in size from ¼ to ⅜ inch.

The face of each tool then can be filed to produce a more intricate design. For example, for tooling a border, file the spike head into a bar ⅜ inch long and then file diagonal lines across the face of the bar. Or punch the face of the bar at intervals with a steel punch. The first tool will make a pattern of diagonal lines, the second a series of raised dots. In tooling a border, successive impressions are made with the tool to form a continuous line.

For tooling backgrounds, file diagonals or punch holes in a square spike head. Filing straight lines across the face of a square tool produces a basket effect. A cross-hatch pattern is created by filing two sets of straight lines at right angles to each other. A fan-shaped head filed with radial lines makes an attractive pattern.

As you file these designs on the spike heads, test them as the work progresses. Dampen a piece of tanned, unfinished leather by stroking it quickly with a wet cloth. Lightly tap the spike head on the leather with a hammer, and observe the result. When a tool produces a design to your satisfaction, cut off the end of the spike, leaving a 3-inch shank—a good length for working leather.

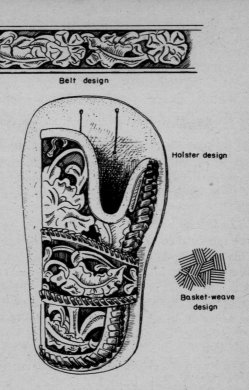

Belt design

Holster design

Basket-weave design

Holster and belt decorated with an abstract leaf design. Detail shows simple basket-weave design created with one tool.

Temporary Buttons

Losing a button on an outdoor trip is a minor annoyance, but it easily can be corrected if you have a needle and thread in your duffel. Temporary buttons can be made from a variety of materials. Here are a few suggestions:

Whittle a button from the end of a pocket comb,

and bore two holes through it by twisting the point of a small knife blade on one side, then the other.

Whittle a button from a thin slab of wood. Take care not to split the wood when making holes with a knife; exert only a gentle pressure on the knife blade. Better yet, heat the end of a piece of wire and burn the holes through the wood—before carving the button, if the wood is delicate.

Shape a button from a piece of thin bone, softened in boiling water for a few minutes.

Cut a piece of stiff leather to shape, punch the holes with a knife, and you have a button.

Emergency Whistle

In the summer, when the sap is flowing in the bark, a willow branch can be whittled into a whistle for calling help in an emergency or for bringing in a hunting dog.

Choose a straight green stem of new-growth willow, about 6 inches long and ½ to ¾ inch in diameter. Cut one end as at A in Figure 1. Then girdle the bark (B) 3 inches from this end. Cut a notch in the end (C) ¼ inch deep.

Now remove the bark, in one piece, between the girdling cut and the notched end. To do this, gently tap the bark around the willow with the handle of your pocketknife, holding the blade between the thumb and fingers. This loosens the bark from the wood. The bark can be removed in one piece by gripping it in the palm of one hand while holding the other end, and twisting it off. It should come off in one piece, as in Figure 2.

The next step is to shave down the section of the willow from the notch to ½ inch from the girdling cut (D in Figure 3). Shave this section to nearly half the

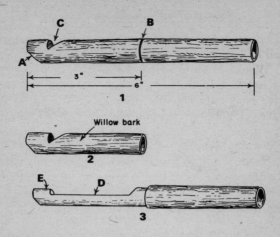

Emergency whistle cut from a willow branch.

willow's diameter, and smooth the surface. This is the whistle's air chamber.

Next, carefully shave a little wood from point E in Figure 3. From here on, it takes a little experimenting to produce a tone. To blow the whistle, wet the wooden part in your mouth and slip on the bark section. The saliva forms a seal between the bark and the wood. Blow through the notched end. If you don't produce a whistle, shave off a little more at point E. Sometimes section D needs a little trimming. Eventually, you should be able to produce a piercing whistle that can be heard far away.

Hooking a Tent Mat from Baling Twine

Few places are colder than the floor of a tent on a frosty morning when you slip out of your sleeping bag. A foot mat between you and the floor is one of the

319

small luxuries that even the hardiest camper will appreciate. Hooking one out of baling twine is a way to pass a rainy morning at camp.

If horses are used at camp, the heavy twine that bales their hay is excellent for hooking a mat. This twine is made of sisal and is very strong.

Whittle the hook for making the mat from a straight, dry limb about ½ inch in diameter and 9 inches long. Remove the bark from one end and scrape the wood smooth. Shave 3 inches of this end down to a diameter of ⅜ inch. Next, cut a notch ⅜ inch from the tip. The drawing shows the correct shape of the notch. When you've cut the notch, taper the end to a rounded point so that it will slip between the loops of the twine.

Gather several lengths of baling twine and tie them together with square knots. Water knots are even

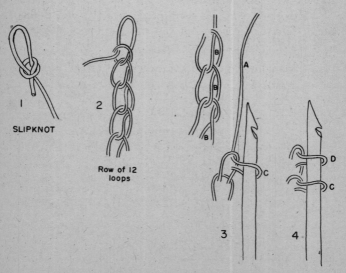

Tent mat is woven around chain of twelve loops.

better. Tie a slip knot in one end (Figure 1). Put the hook through the loop of the slip knot, grab the running end in the notch, and once more pull it through the loop. Repeat this procedure twelve times, until you have a chain of loops (Figure 2). The mat is woven around these loops by repeating a basic stitch.

As work proceeds around the loops, the hook will always be in one loop and there will be a running end (A in Figure 3) of twine. The hook, having made loop C, goes through that part of the adjacent loop, B, grasps the running end, A, and pulls it through loop B to form loop D (Figure 4). There are now two loops on the hook.

With both loops C and D on its shank, the hook grasps running end A again, and pulls it through both loops C and D, forming the equivalent of another loop C. The hook then goes down through the *next* loop B, and the work continues.

This basic stitch is continued until the mat is finished. The twine is tied at the completion of the mat so it won't unravel.

Index